What people are sa… "Where Roots Grow Deep"

Bob Welch is destined to become America's most beloved writer on the family.

—MIKE YORKEY, author and former *Focus on the Family* editor

With experiences as vivid and universal as Angela's Ashes, Where Roots Grow Deep *does more than bring substance to the image of family. It encourages reconnection. It makes us want to touch the world and change the way we'll be remembered in it. It tells us how we can. And Welch does it without a single word of dogma, no preaching, no "thou shalts" but with stories of lived faith that fall as quietly as leaves against the forest floor...*

—NOVELIST JANE KIRKPATRICK

Bob Welch is a master storyteller. Where Roots Grow Deep *is a collection of stories that stirred my heart, enlightened my mind, and, most of all, caused me to want to pass on powerful life-legacies to those I love.*

—STEVE MCVEY, author and president of *Grace Walk* Ministries

Any reader will sense the rhythm of life as told through simple yet profound stories of a deeply spiritual family lived day by day and generation by generation.

—THE HON. SEN. MARK O. HATFIELD

Welch is a gifted artist with words, a thoughtful analyst of the human condition, and an authentic person who shares stories that satisfy our thirsting for truth and relevance. Where Roots Grow Deep *is a book that paints for us the longing of our hearts for how we want life to be, and gives us hope and encouragement to make it that way.*

—RICK TAYLOR, pastor, author, and Family Life speaker

Bob Welch is a creative, engaging, humorous writer who sees heartwarming stories in such mundane things as running relays, electric football games, digital alarm clocks, and work boots. His compelling storytelling-style shines once again in this book of family trees and family legacies.

—KERBY ANDERSON, President,
Probe Ministries

Need encouragement that today's actions really do matter? Then Bob Welch's reminders of the power of intergenerational relationships are for you. Filled with wisdom and hope, his stories offer fresh insight into what makes families work.

—AUTHOR SANDRA ALDRICH

WHERE ROOTS GROW DEEP

Bob Welch

HARVEST HOUSE PUBLISHERS
Eugene, Oregon 97402

Cover by Left Coast Design, Portland, Oregon

To Contact the Author

Write to:

409 Sunshine Acres Dr.
Eugene, OR 97401

or send e-mail to:

bwelch1@concentric.net

WHERE ROOTS GROW DEEP

Published by Harvest House Publishers
Eugene, Oregon 97402

Library of Congress Cataloging-in-Publication Data

Welch, Bob, 1954-
Where roots grow deep / by Bob Welch.
p. cm.
ISBN 0-7369-0027-6
1. Family—Oregon. 2. Intergenerational relations—Oregon.
I. Title.
HQ536.15.O7W45 1999 99-21702
306.85'09795—dc21 CIP

Printed in the United States of America.

To the memory of Gram and Pop,
Grandpa Schu, and all the other ancestors
whose legacy trees I'm privileged
to share, with thanks for
passing on faith, hope, and love.

Acknowledgments

With deep appreciation to:

- My sister-in-law Ann Petersen, for first reading this manuscript and then so deftly picking the good fruit from the bad.
- Nancy Shattuck-Smallwood, for editorial pruning that gave shape to a once-shabby tree.
- My mother, Marolyn, for stories of her father and sideline cheering for her son.
- Bonnie and Harold Youngberg, for passing on an honorable legacy that, not incidentally, includes my wife.
- My sister- and brother-in-law, Linda and Greg Scandrett, for faith leaves that have stayed green through the most devastating of droughts.
- My sister, Linda Crew, for the e-mail encouragement of a fellow writer and for stretching my imagination with all those childhood games of "quicksand boat."
- Uncles Glenn Klein and Bill Welch, for their valuing of children and their vision to see beyond the now.
- Janet Bain, Grayce Coffey, Kim and Michele Wofford, Christy Kintigh, and Ron Hood, for memories of The Farm; and Jeanne and Wayne Hood, for hospitality on my return visit to it.
- My editor at Harvest House, Terry Glaspey, for sharing my love of words and caring enough to occasionally ask me for better ones.
- Novelist Jane Kirkpatrick, for inspiring her former mentor to reach higher and get up waaaaay earlier.
- David and Steve Austin, Oscar Hernandez, Bob and Margaret Kintigh, Marvin and Dana Kropf, Leighanne Sager, Pat Taylor, and Arie and Lynn Van Wingerden, for taking time to share their stories.
- My son Ryan, for the wisdom to follow my footsteps—and sometimes not.
- My son Jason, who sat next to me throughout most of this book's creation, for muffling his cheers when his computer football team would score.
- My wife and best friend, Sally, for allowing me a limb on her family tree, for her deep appreciation of the people and places in her past, and for loving me even though I wasn't a farmer.
- God, whose grace soothes us like the shade of an apple tree on a sweltering afternoon.

Contents

V. Losing Leaves

VI. Scattering Seeds Anew

But blessed is the man who trusts in the LORD, *whose confidence is in him. He will be like a tree planted by the water that sends out its roots by the stream. It does not fear when heat comes; its leaves are always green. It has no worries in a year of drought and never fails to bear fruit.*

—Jeremiah 17:7

legacy-*n.*, something received from an ancestor or predecessor or from the past.

—*Webster's Ninth*
New Collegiate Dictionary

Introduction

> The principle of stability dominates. It dominates by means of an ever-recurring cycle... repeating itself silently and ceaselessly...constituted of the successive and repeated processes of birth, growth, maturity, death, and decay. Death supersedes life and life rises again from what is dead.
>
> —*The Soil and Health: A Study of Organic Agriculture*

Sitting in the country church, we all knew this time would come. Knew it would come in the same way Gram, stepping onto the rutted planks of the porch on a frosty fall morning, knew it was time to cut back the roses, cover the bulbs with a maple-leaf blanket, and start gathering walnuts to give to the grandkids for Christmas; winter would soon be here.

At 95, she had outlasted Pop by more than a decade. She had spent three years alone on the farm. Then she had moved to a retirement home in town that was nice but never home. Home was a 105-year-old farmhouse in which her father-in-law's initials were still faintly etched in the cement walkway: *Nels B. Youngberg, 1912.* In which she and Pop had risen early to feed the chickens and milk the cows, and watched summer sunsets perform on the Coast Range stage. In which the two had lived for more than six decades, their shapes imprinted in their mattress like a couple of flutes on a pie crust.

She died early on the morning of October 30, 1997: Louise Skinner Youngberg, the grandmother of my wife; Sally's last grandparent to die.

The next morning my mother called. Her voice was soft and measured, and I knew something was wrong. Only hours ago, she told me, my grandfather had died. Benjamin F. Schumacher, 98, was *my* last grandparent to die.

A few days later, as Sally and I sat in the country church in tiny Carlton, Oregon, awaiting the start of Gram's memorial service, I realized that these back-to-back deaths had suddenly ended a century-long generation of our two families; each of us had now lost all four of our grandparents.

When I was ten years old, we had spent Thanksgiving with my uncle and his family in their house surrounded by majestic oak trees. We awoke to a world of white, an unexpected heavy snowfall having come in the night. But we quickly discovered the painful price of this beauty: Huge branches from the trees had snapped under the weight of the heavy, wet snow, barely missing the house. The oaks looked fragile and incomplete.

Now, decades later, the weight of time had become too much for our family trees. In 24 hours, two main branches had snapped and fallen. And that's how our two families looked to me as I sat in that church: fragile and incomplete.

For my family, Grandpa Schu, as we called him, was our rock; as a boy, I had sweated and learned alongside the man for three memorable summers of grounds-keeping. For Sally's family, Gram had been the hinge on which the screen door swung, a woman of remarkable simplicity and yet uncommon depth.

But when Greg Scandrett—a pastor, friend and brother-in-law—stood up front and talked about Gram, he said something that soothed my sorrow about both deaths. Something that reminded me of continuity, not conclusion; hope, not hopelessness.

"We are Gram's legacy," he said, his eyes sweeping the pews in which most of the hundred or so people were related to the woman. "We are what's left to show the world who she was."

In a small church in rural Oregon, his words were simple and yet profound, a reminder that the passing on of faith, hope, and love from one generation to another generation is honorable and important. And yet in today's culture, such thinking has become voice-in-the-wilderness stuff.

A recent *Newsweek* magazine cover featured an author whose book *The Nurture Assumption* not only suggests family legacies are irrelevant, but that parents are, too; they have, she contends, little influence on who their own children become as adults. Hollywood has essentially written the extended family out of the script, Walton's Mountain having been replaced by Melrose Place. Washington, DC, offers the family terms of endearment, but not much walk to back the talk. And in mainstream America, where most of us live, apathy eats away at family trees with the quiet commitment of a bark beetle.

My wife, Sally, a receptionist at a pediatrics clinic, brings home stories of children who can't trace their family tree to even their father—and this in a university community that people routinely call "progressive." Occasionally, the cases of abuse are so atrocious that doctors cry; once a cop broke down right in the office. But most of what she sees is parents and children who seem dreadfully disconnected. Occasionally, young mothers will scratch out the phrase "Child's Father" on the registration form and scrawl "not applicable."

At one time, I believe, people knew and understood the value of intergenerational links. But the cultural clatter has drowned out the message; it's hard to appreciate the past and prepare for the future in a world that beckons us to live for only the now.

"To live for the moment is the prevailing passion—to live for yourself, not for your predecessors or posterity," writes Christopher Lasch in *The Culture of Narcissism.* "We are fast losing the sense of historical continuity, the sense of belonging to a succession of generations originating in the past and stretching into the future."

This book, I hope, inspires introspection, whispers encouragement, and gently challenges us all to consider how the world will remember us once we're gone. It suggests fathers—and mothers—are not only "applicable," but integral. It suggests children are a privilege to have. Finally, it suggests some of us inherit rich legacies, others ragtag legacies, but we all wear hand-me-downs.

For those of you who have been blessed, I hope this book encourages you to multiply those blessings and pass them on. For those of you who have not, I hope this book encourages you to begin a legacy of your own. We are all inextricably linked to our pasts. Studies show that "the sins of the father" commonly visit generations that follow—but we are not slaves to those pasts.

Occasionally, you'll see a reference to what I call the "legacy tree." That phrase, rather than "family tree," might more accurately reflect this book's focus: a dynamic, perpetual process, not names frozen in time. Legacies are active, not static. If a "family tree" speaks of fill-in-the-blank infrastructure—a genealogical roster of who played on this team and when—a legacy tree speaks of action—the stories of who contributed what to the team's cause.

Legacies are that place where those who have gone before us still make a difference. Where values are passed on from one generation to the next. Where roots grow deep.

They play out in many forms. They can be physical, like the 1905 baseball journal written by my then-17-year-old grandfather that was passed on to my father and ultimately to me. They can be spiritual. They can be a number of things—from a name to a business, from traditions to acres of trees, from a way of living life to a way of making apple crisp.

They are transferred in many ways—through words in a will, genes in a body, numbers in a bank account, even the umbilical cord of a crack-addicted mother. But the legacies God honors highest are legacies of the heart, and these are best transferred by how we live our lives...by example. "Man looks at the outward appearance," says 1 Samuel 16:7, "but the LORD looks at the heart." In such soil are the legacies in this book rooted.

I've been blessed to live most of my life in Oregon, where trees dominate the state's physical, historic, economic, and recreational landscape. We have more timberland and produce more Christmas trees than any state in the union. Some of the world's largest trees—not to mention my prized six-foot dogwood—grow here.

I've climbed trees, camped beneath them, run through forests of them, photographed them, pruned them, written stories about loggers nearly killed by them, ricocheted golf balls off them, and sawed them (the 14 stitches in my left thigh evidence that, at least on one occasion, I've even sawed *beyond* them). Thus, when I decided to write about families and legacies, trees seemed the appropriate metaphor on which to hang a theme. "In the woods," wrote Thoreau, "we return to reason and faith." Scripture uses trees in all sorts of ways to enlighten us with truth; they represent life, faith, wisdom.

I'm amazed that a single seed of a giant sequoia—a seed the size of a corn nut—stores the genetic material that can become the planet's most massive living thing (California is home to a giant sequoia that weighs more than 6167 tons, the equivalent of 740 elephants).

Massive and as seemingly indestructible as that tree might seem, it will die someday. But when it falls, though it may leave an empty spot in that forest, it will also leave a legacy. It will become humus—a thick layer of rotted trunks and branches, decaying ferns, mushrooms, and animal corpses. This forest compost will nurture the next generation and sustain yet another seed the size of a corn nut, as part of the "ever-recurring cycle…repeating itself silently and ceaselessly…through birth, growth, maturity, death, and decay."

In the same way, *Where Roots Grow Deep* explores the phases of intergenerational families in terms of scattering seeds, sinking roots, branching out, weathering time, losing leaves, and scattering seeds anew.

Like my previous book, *A Father for All Seasons,* this one is less a sociological overview than a collection of grass-roots stories. It relies on the experiences of those who are part of my own legacy tree, those I've encountered in more than 20 years as a journalist, and those I've met through other means.

Though proud of the families of which I'm a part, I don't hold them up—nor do I hold myself up—as a standard of perfection. Instead, I offer my stories and their stories as a means of unlocking your own. For we all have grandeur in our midst, if only we will take time to look.

Not long ago, for example, my sister-in-law, Linda, stood in front of a church and told about losing her 16-year-old son, and how legacies inherited from her parents and grandparents had helped sustain her. She ended her talk with a question that I hope this book coaxes us all to consider.

"We all will leave legacies," she said. "The question is, what kind?"

Scattering Seeds

Of Needs and Wants

> Seeds are the archetypal beginning, the unit of being. Sometimes they are so small one can hardly see them.
>
> —*Bringing a Garden to Life*

To some degree, each of us is a collage created by those who went on before us; we, in turn, help create the collage of those who follow. We are each works in process, none of us ever really finished.

Unlike a lifeless collage, however, we may respond to the process; in fact, *how* we respond plays a big part in who we become. As this collage is taking shape, sometimes we might get an artistic touch that, at the time, doesn't seem right to us. Sometimes we might get a dash of color here that we think unnecessary, a shape there that we resist.

Though we may not want that addition, we may need that addition. I believe it has something to do with love and grace—and whether we accept such artistic touches when they're offered.

I was 13. It was 1967, the year I started hanging around with a handful of kids a grade older than I was. The year I learned to smoke and swear. The year my baseball coach told us to take a lap around Cloverland Park and, halfway around, a bunch of us just quit and walked. The previous year, I had made the Age 12-13 All-Star Team as a rookie. This year, as a "veteran," I not only wouldn't make that team, but I wouldn't seem to care about *not* making it.

Around me, the revolutionary sixties swirled, ushering in an invitation to freedom, to experimentation, to breaking away from the shackles of authority and boldly going one's own way. I was poised for a summer of nothingness, the idea of irresponsibility happily wallowing in my teenage brain.

At this point I learned that my mother, in all her wisdom and foresight, had arranged for me to spend the next ten weeks mowing a fraternity lawn with her father—my grandfather, the ex-Army officer.

"Now, Bob," he said, looking at me and my tattered tennis shoes on the first day of work, "what you really need is a good pair of work boots."

What I really needed, I felt, was to be back in bed, not mowing a lawn the size of Arlington National Cemetery in 90-degree heat while being watched by Sergeant Perfectionist. This lawn job, you see, was not some here-and-gone task that could be completed whenever I had a spare couple of hours. This was a full-time job. I was expected to show up virtually every day at 8 A.M. (not to be confused with 8:05 A.M.) and complete a list of jobs that my grandfather had written on 3"x 5" index cards while devising his battle plan the previous night: mowing, edging, watering, weeding, fertilizing, sweeping, pruning, planting, trimming, painting, sanding, scraping, taping, chipping, and clipping.

For this, I was to be paid $1.50 an hour.

Boots? "Get real," I wanted to tell the old man. It was bad enough that I would be spending my summer trying to scrape unwanted grass from sidewalk cracks, but did I have to wear a ball and chain in the process? Boots restricted. Boots were clunky and time-consuming. But more importantly, in the mind of a 13-year-old boy who was knocking on the door of sixties coolness, boots simply looked, well, stupid.

From the beginning, it was clear that my grandfather and I were separated by more than two generations (more like two universes). We saw the world differently. We saw this job differently. We saw proper work attire differently. He showed up each morning in a uniform that was part U.S. Army, part *Home & Garden:* well-pressed beige pants with cuffs, a long-sleeve shirt often buttoned at the top, an Oregon State University baseball hat and, of course, boots. Well-oiled boots.

At 68 and retired, Benjamin Franklin Schumacher presided over the grounds of the hallowed Sigma Alpha Epsilon fraternity at Oregon State University (OSU), where he was treasurer and self-appointed guardian of the grounds. To him, this was not a fraternity. It was a block-wide, split-level shrine. Nearly half a century before, at what had then been known as Oregon Agricultural College, he had joined the Sigma Alpha Epsilons (SAEs). After college, he had continued to be involved in the fraternity, becoming affectionately known around town as Schu of '22. In the years after World War II, my father and uncle had been SAEs here, too, which only added to my burden.

To my grandfather, this was not a collection of grass, shrubs, and bark dust. This was sacred ground, as if he were the high priest of pruning and peat moss, and I were his acolyte—albeit an acolyte in cutoffs and scruffy black Converse All-Stars, practically the only tennis shoe available back then.

"Now, Bob," he once said, "tell that daughter of mine—that's your mom, you know—that she should invest in some good boots for you. Get the ones with the steel-shanked toes. They'll protect you." Then he laughed his *hey-hey-hey* laugh, a kind of laugh that sounded like a lawn mower that sputtered but wouldn't turn off, even when you hit the stop button.

Yeah, yeah, yeah.

The fraternity sat on the corner of 29th and Harrison, two fairly busy streets in the college town of Corvallis, and all the more reason Sergeant Schumacher wanted the lawn to be billiard-table green, the sidewalks swept, the hedges trimmed, the fruit wormless in his beloved apple trees along 30th Street.

Needless to say, he wasn't all that pleased when I over-fertilized the Harrison Street Quadrant and the grass turned the color of beef Stroganoff; nor when, upon returning from a weekend camping trip, I realized I had accidentally left on the sprinklers for three solid days and created Fraternity Lake. But as the days on the job turned into weeks on the job, I noticed something about the man: He never got mad at me.

"I'll tell ya, Bob, nobody's perfect," he said after the sprinkler incident. Instead of berating me for doing something wrong, he would simply take whatever tool I had used inappropriately and show me how to use it right.

When you do a task, he would say, do it as well as you can, even if nobody is watching. When you try to fix something and find yourself stuck, improvise; use your imagination. When you take out a weed, get the whole root or "the guy" will be back in a few weeks.

(He always talked about weeds as if they were human and part of some sort of top-secret military operation, as if dandelions had generals who devised intricate plans to invade and capture, say, Eastern Arborvitae.)

He led; I followed. While I did my work, he did his. Only when he did his work, it was with a certain enthusiasm that I couldn't muster, as if he found a deeper purpose to the job than mowing, weeding, and trimming. As the day heated up, he would sweat an old man's sweat, sometimes pulling out a handkerchief from his back pocket and wiping his forehead and neck, but never complaining. "Work before play," he would say. "Work before play."

One day, when I was changing the southeast sprinklers, a guy in a car turned onto Harrison Street, rolled down his window, and said, "Hey, looks great."

After he drove on, I looked at the landscaping and realized the man was right. It did look great. I realized people actually noticed the job we were doing here. I realized, as deeply as a 13-year-old can realize, that I was somehow part of something. Something good.

Gradually, I began caring about how the SAE place looked almost as much as Schu did. I learned to raise the wheels of the mower on uneven ground to prevent the blade from leaving scars. When an adjustment lever snapped off one of our rotating sprinkler heads, I learned to improvise with a paper clip. And when going after weeds, I not only learned to get individual roots, but flushed out entire platoons.

For three summers, I helped my grandfather take care of the SAE grounds, and came to believe ours was the best-kept fraternity or sorority in Corvallis, probably in the entire world. But I learned more than how to keep grass green, sidewalks swept, and trees trimmed. I learned that work was good and honorable. I learned that what something looked like on the outside said a lot about what it was like on the inside. I learned there was a right way and a wrong way to do something.

More than anything, I learned how to grow up. To care more and swear less. Just like the Gravenstein apple trees along 30th Street needed pruning so the fruit would be better, so did I need some pruning, Schu figured. And he was right.

But finally, my stint at the SAE house ended. I made a career advancement, going to work raking beans and packing strawberries in a cannery with a mouth-watering salary—$2.50 an hour—and unbeatable fringe benefits: a pop machine and the pleasant smell of a nearby Chinese restaurant.

In February of my sophomore year in high school, I was sitting in Mrs. Shaw's English class when an office worker brought me a pink-slip message. All eyes turned to me. My heart pounded. It read: "Your grandfather is waiting for you in the office."

My father was dead. My mother was dead. The possibilities swirled in my mind as I hurried down the hall to the office. There stood my grandfather. Nobody was dead.

"Now, Bob," he said, "I've arranged to take you out of school for a short time."

I asked why.

"Let's just say it's a little birthday surprise," he said, laughing with his *hey-hey-hey* laugh. We got into his gold Oldsmobile, which was roughly the size of the *USS Teddy Roosevelt,* and drove down Buchanan Street a mile to a one-stop shopping store. I slumped low so nobody would see me.

I couldn't figure out what was going on, but he led so I followed him into the store. We stopped in the sporting-goods section.

Some kids get cars on their sixteenth birthday. Some get stereos or ten-speed bikes or skis or skateboards. But in 1970, when I turned 16, my grandfather cared too much to give me something I wanted. Instead, he gave me something I needed.

"Now, Bob," he said, "take your pick." And he gestured toward a huge display of work boots, the kind with the steel-shanked toes.

Faith and Imagination

> If planting a seed is an act of faith and imagination, planting a tree is even more so. The effects on the landscape will be defining, and will be seen for a long time.
>
> —*Bringing a Garden to Life*

It is 2 A.M., and in the farmland east of Portland, Oregon, I am running alone on a dark country road with only a small flashlight in hand. Suddenly, I hear them: footsteps from behind. Faint at first, they get louder and louder until it happens: I am passed by another runner with a small flashlight in hand—a runner who then fades into the darkness ahead of me.

Once again, I am alone, just another of the 10,500 participants in the largest running-relay race in the world, the Hood to Coast event stretching 196 miles from Timberline Lodge at Mount Hood (elevation 6000 feet) to a city called Seaside on the Pacific Ocean (elevation 0).

Carrying on a legacy is like running the Hood to Coast Relay: It doesn't really matter who passes you or who you pass; everyone starts at different times. What really matters is simply how well you run your leg.

Carrying on a legacy is *unlike* running the Hood to Coast Relay in that you get to take a shower, you don't spend most of the time cooped up with five sweaty runners in a van that smells like a locker room last cleaned in 1957, and you don't have to wait up to half an hour to use the Port-a-potty.

Before I draw any more parallels between life's legacies and running's lunatics, let me explain this event more thoroughly. Each Hood to Coast team consists of 12 members. Each team—there were 875 in 1997—has a name (a straightforward, thoughtful name such as the Original Roads Scholars—our team, Slugs R Us, Show Me the Moleskin, Gordon Lightfoot, Start Slow and Taper Off, Kwitcherbellyakin II, and 12 Dips in the Road).

Individuals each run three legs that are about five miles in length, handing a Velcro wrist bracelet to the person running next. Teams travel in two vans, leapfrogging down the road to drop off and pick up runners.

Finding your just-finished runner at one of the exchange points is a little like finding a friend whose flight has just landed at O'Hare International—except in the Hood to Coast, you have no clue which flight he or she has arrived on.

But here's another way carrying on a legacy and running in the relay are alike: Each runner on your team faces a different challenge. For some, it's Friday night's knee-pounding, 2000-foot elevation drop from the starting line at Timberline Lodge to the next exchange point 5.6 miles away; for others, it's the somewhat scary legs that weave through the warehouse district of Portland—for our team, usually in the dead of night; and for still others, it's the 500-foot climb up a twisting gravel road in the Coast Range in Saturday's heat.

Runners catch a couple hours of sleep here and there, usually in fields or parking lots, and try to survive something more challenging than the running itself: the smell in the van, an odd combination of sweat, dust, exhaust, socks, Vaseline, and rotten banana peels.

It's awesome.

When you arrive at the beach—for the fastest teams, that means in about 16 hours, though our team is still struggling to break the coveted "sub-day" mark—you feel this wonderful blend of exhaustion and exhilaration. You feel like showering, eating three large pizzas, and sleeping—all at once. But best of all, you feel like you've been part of something good and noble, regardless of how many teams finished ahead of or behind you.

The exhilaration stems, in part, from a sense of belonging. Of contributing to something greater than yourself. Of feeling a sense of being *necessary,* as if you not only experienced, but also helped create some sort of shared history.

Just like in real life. We're each part of a legacy tree—a tree whose health or lack thereof we will influence. Just as runners take that bracelet and hand off that bracelet, so do we inherit a legacy and pass on a legacy.

Frankly, we have no choice; legacies are passed on like a boat leaves a wake.

Another thing: The legacies we ultimately leave don't begin once we die; they begin once we're born. For who we are as a person is what we leave as a person.

My friend Nancy, the mother of two young daughters, rarely gets ruffled around her girls. Ask her why, and she tells the story of being a little girl herself, hanging on her father's favorite tree. And how, suddenly, the branch snapped. She was not hurt, but the branch was splintered and barely hung from the trunk.

All day long, she worried about her father coming home. She feared he would be angry; after all, this was no ordinary tree. She feared she would be punished. But when her father came home, he wasn't angry. Instead, he gathered together some tar and rags, took Nancy out to the tree and, like an amateur tree surgeon, set the "broken arm." The limb continued to grow. And Nancy learned a lesson that she's never forgotten.

"To my father, the tree limb was just a 'thing,'" she says, looking back. "I was more important to him. And so when something breaks or goes wrong around the girls, I find myself remembering his example. A toy is just a *thing*. But my daughters are"—and her eyes light up—"my daughters."

Legacies come in all sorts of forms. Some lean toward the practical, some toward the heart. An uncle of mine and an uncle of Sally's have made contributions to our sons' college education; that's leaving a legacy.

My in-laws have provided immeasurable counsel on major financial decisions we've made (a lifesaver for a financially impaired guy like me); that's leaving a legacy.

Modeling. Teaching. Inspiring. Challenging. All are ways of transferring legacies from one generation to the next. So are gift-giving. Advice-offering. Letter-writing. Hand-holding. Baseball-throwing. And cookie-baking.

What we give depends largely on what we're willing to sacrifice; it's the same way in the race.

Perspective is important, too. I need to remember I'm part of a team; others are depending on me. If I take that bracelet with no sense of purpose, I'm—as runners affectionately call a plodder who gets passed—"road kill."

But if commitment and perspective are necessary ingredients to running the good race, so are a couple of less obvious factors: faith and imagination.

Once I've begun my leg, the van driver begins his. He or she must pass me along the road, wind through miles and miles of vans, and get the next runner in position for the handoff from me. As I run, I'm unsure whether the next runner will be waiting for me; I simply must trust.

Finally, the quality of my effort depends on imagination. One year, I drew one of the toughest legs: the gravel-road uphiller in Saturday's heat. The only thing that kept me going was remembering that the pain was only temporary.

Visualizing my teammates awaiting my arrival. Imagining the smell of the surf at Seaside on Saturday evening.

In the same way, legacies require the imagination to see not what is, but *what could be*. To realize our children are not going to always be just "our children" but other people's husbands and wives and, eventually, someone's father or mother or teacher or pastor or lunar module mechanic.

We reap what we sow. In the Hood to Coast, the fruit bursts forth when the runners in Van No. 1 meet up with the runners in Van No. 2 on the sand at Seaside—a virtual family reunion in which you share stories of your respective journeys, congratulate one another, and realize the pain was all worth it.

In Big Life, it comes when your son e-mails you that he's really developing an interest in photography, and you think of your once-teenage father, back in the thirties, souping prints in his basement darkroom.

It comes when your wife decorates the set for your church's Christmas program at the city's civic auditorium, and her mother-the-accomplished-home-decorator is on hand to see what her daughter has done.

It comes when your sister-the-former-thespian watches her twins light up the audience in *Oliver.*

It comes when your recently widowed mother, while watching her grandsons in a basketball game, offers one of the most poignant halftime analyses you've ever heard: "When I see Ryan and Jason out there, I say to myself,: 'These are Warren's legacies. Without him, they wouldn't be here.'"

These are your "Seaside moments," when you realize there is payback for the pain. Perhaps you haven't run the perfect race; none of us ever will. Nevertheless, you've done your part to keep that bracelet going. And part of you goes with it: down the mountain, through the city, and faithfully into the darkness ahead.

Gifty

> Grafting involves the transfer of a scion, or twig of a desired variety to be propagated, to the stock or seedling plant which supplies the roots of the new plant. When the actively growing tissue of the scion is brought into proper contact with similar growing tissue of the stock, they unite, heal and grow as one tree.
>
> —*1001 Questions Answered About Trees*

They stood together in a bamboo-sided church in Africa, a middle-aged man and his wife, the only two white faces of the couple hundred people in attendance. They held a child, whose skin was dark like those in the circle of people surrounding them.

Here, on a hot, dark evening in March 1996, a ceremony of promise took place on a Liberian landscape seared by civil war. Once only hours from death, a four-year-old Liberian girl was being given new life. She was being handed over to her adoptive parents, Marvin and Dana Kropf, whose home in Oregon was literally halfway around the world.

The little girl's name was Gifty. It was a name given her by Mother Hannah, the head of the orphanage that had been her refuge until the Kropfs came forth. It meant "gift of God."

The elders of the nondenominational Christian church placed their hands on the threesome and prayed for their safety. They commissioned Marvin and Dana, giving them a solemn charge to take care of Gifty, to raise her for God's glory. They lavished the couple with handmade garments—part of this "gowning" ceremony. For Dana: a wraparound skirt, a blouse, and a "lapa" that tied around the top of the skirt. For Marvin: an embroidered shirt and a fez-shaped hat to match. When you return, the elders joked, perhaps you will get pants.

As the ceremony continued, the Kropfs found themselves immersed in emotion: Here they stood, a couple who had four biological children of their own, watching the culmination of years of prayer and persistence. In split-second flashbacks, Dana found herself remembering all that had led to this moment, this inheritance of a little girl who once was nothing but a wallet-sized photo on the Kropf family refrigerator.

In December 1989, a group of dissidents lit the fuse of war against the Liberian government. An ill-trained rebel army spread pain and suffering across the country that sits on the west coast of Africa, killing, torturing, and raping at will. In the span of eight years, they fueled a civil war that would drive more than half of the 2.3 million pre-war population from their homes, kill more than 150,000 people—nearly three times the number of troops the United States lost in Vietnam—and ruin the country's economy.

But in a world with its eye on other atrocities such as Bosnia and Rwanda, Liberia rarely made CNN. So the world didn't hear much about the civilians being killed. Didn't hear much about children being killed. Didn't hear much about how the rebel soldiers would see a pregnant woman, place bets on whether her child was a boy or girl, then slice her open to see who had won.

A year after the civil war began, a young woman just outside the capital city of Monrovia became pregnant. She was nine months along and due soon when attacked by the rebels. A priest, on his ambulance rounds to recover victims of war, saw her from a distance: a crumpled body alongside a road.

At first the scene evoked only the wretched redundancy of war—a young woman slain by men with seemingly no consciences. But as he approached the scene, he was startled to see movement beside the lifeless body.

It was a baby. Alive.

❧ ❧ ❧

Appropriately enough, it was Mother's Day when Dana first felt the tug. A man from African Christian Fellowship International spoke at Family Bible Church in rural Brownsville, Oregon, that day, and Dana and Marvin were moved by what they heard. It was 1994.

The man told of the horrors of war in his homeland. Of there being a price on his head because he dared to blow the whistle on those who splintered families with the pull of a trigger or the stab of a knife. Of cannibalism, executions, and children orphaned by war.

It was a world as far away from the Kropfs' existence as the 8000 miles between the two places. They lived in the pastoral farmland of Oregon's Willamette Valley, in an area heavily sprinkled with Mennonite families. Marvin ran a feed business whose warehouse and office were just down the road from their house. Dana had a cake-decorating business and dabbled in crafts.

When the speaker spoke of children being killed, though, Dana looked down the pew at their two-year-old daughter,

Suzanne. She and Marvin also had a 15-year-old son, Jeremy; a 19-year-old daughter, Deb; and a 20-year-old son, Matt. But the orphaned children of whom the man spoke were nearer Suzanne's age than the others, and on this Sunday morning, Dana thought of what it must be like for those children.

That day, she and Marvin decided to sponsor a child and send money to help keep him or her fed and clothed. The child they chose was a little girl who had never known a mother or father. Her name, it turned out, was Gifty.

The Kropfs took the 1"x 1" photo, had it enlarged at a copy shop, and stuck it to their refrigerator. Each month, they dutifully sent their money. Marvin even worked with the man from African Christian Fellowship International to send grain to the country in need.

Eventually, it just seemed like the right question to ask: Was Gifty available for adoption? It was possible, yes, the man told them, but not easy, or inexpensive, or even safe.

But adoption had been part of Dana and Marvin's heritage. Marvin had a number of adopted nephews and nieces. When Dana was seven, her parents were set to adopt a Korean baby when a crop failure canceled the decision; but like a seed, the idea had been planted in Dana's heart.

On one hand, it made no sense: The Kropfs already had a family. They had security. And they had a business to rebuild; a fire later in 1994 had leveled the warehouse and mill, seriously injuring three workers.

But in June 1995, the Kropfs said yes to Gifty. The process made rebuilding the family business look easy. Basic communication with those in a country torn by war was almost impossible; mail service didn't exist. The Morovian International Airport had been destroyed. All the Kropfs had were a few contacts—names sketched on napkins—and a lot of prayers.

Liberia, Dana tells you, is a different world. A world where the Kropfs once lost phone contact for two weeks.

Where you can get high-centered on some jungle road and not be seen for weeks.

While Marvin worked on getting the mill warehouse and mill back in business, Dana worked on getting Gifty to Oregon. Working with Plan Loving Adoption Now out of McMinnville, Oregon, she filled out forms. Made dozens of phone calls. Cultivated a stack of paperwork that grew like corn in July.

Finally, it was settled. With the civil war winding down, Marvin and Dana would go to Africa to pick up Gifty: Eugene to San Francisco to New York to Brussels to Sierra Leone, a country which borders Liberia to the north. Three days of travel, 12,000 dollars worth of expenses, all for the live version of the little girl whose picture was on the refrigerator.

When they arrived in Sierra Leone, nobody was there to meet the Kropfs as they expected. They took a small plane into a primitive airport in Liberia. When they got off, they saw a man with a sign that said: "Mr. and Mrs. Kropf."

"Come," said the man, "Gifty is waiting."

They found her sitting on a wooden bench, looking almost doll-like, her jet-black hair ablaze with colored ribbons. She lifted her arms and smiled.

In Liberia, crying is not something you do in public; it is a cultural taboo. But on that day, in a country where war had left a legacy of pain, tears of joy slipped down the faces of two people.

Gifty is believed to have been the first child adopted out of Liberia after the civil war, according to the agency that helped it happen. But to those who circled the Kropfs in love that evening, she was more than a historical footnote.

She was a treasure belonging to them all. For in Liberia, the village-to-raise-a-child slogan is not a book title or the politically correct slogan of the month—it is truth. The Kropfs noticed that from the moment they arrived. Noticed it when Gifty was writing on a white-painted wall with a piece of charcoal and a young man gently but firmly told her to stop. Noticed it when seeing mothers leave their children, knowing that neighbors would dutifully watch them. Much different from America, the Kropfs realized.

In Liberia, says Dana, children are considered a national treasure. They are an integral part of the fabric of life. They're not dropped off at day care; they go everywhere their parents go and, when left behind, are cared for by others. In church they can sing every song, shuffle every dance step.

And so it was that at the farewell ceremony, children, too, joined in. The elders prayed and blessed this new trio, bestowing upon Marvin and Dana the names of the Kru tribe to which Gifty belonged: Marvin was given the name Jolatoh ("End of the war") and Dana, Juahdee ("Mother of many").

In the hot African night, they held tightly to their gift. For they knew they had become the hands of hope for a people with little. And the door to the future for a child who once had none.

Pop

> Witness trees are trees referred to in old land deeds. They were blazed with a marking that corresponded to a nearby square corner post used in land survey....Sometimes the marking was buried by later growth, but when this was cut away, the original inscription appeared.
>
> —*1001 Questions Answered About Trees*

On a windy hill above a patchwork quilt of barns, orchards, and freshly plowed fields, they buried Pop Youngberg. He's not famous like the little girl who grew up on a farm just five miles away: children's author Beverly Cleary. In fact, beyond his family (he's my wife's grandfather) and the folks of Yamhill County, few ever heard of the man. His obituary isn't particularly impressive. He never was president of this or on the board of that.

But he needs to be remembered. For the Pop Youngbergs of the world are a vanishing breed, and our fast-and-frantic world can learn from their legacies, obscure though they may be.

In a time when Americans are more mobile than ever, Pop died in the same house in which he was born 89 years earlier. Most Americans will hold numerous jobs in their lifetime. Pop held one: farmer. Some marriages won't outlast the life of the family refrigerator. Pop and his wife were married 60 years.

To Pop, life was a simple trilogy of tilling the earth below him, worshiping the God above him, and loving the family around him.

His life would seem to be monotonous: plowing, seeding, fertilizing, and harvesting 125 acres on a turtle-slow tractor. But he embraced farming as something good and natural and honorable. Years after he was too old to even walk to the chicken coop, he still awoke at dawn, ready to begin the daily chores.

He never had a business card, never got a promotion, and rarely took a vacation. But like his Swedish parents who tilled the same soil, he loved the family farm with a quiet passion and knew that that's where he must die—in the white house flanked by the giant maple tree at the end of the long gravel lane.

Three weeks before his death, his words came slowly and with great strain. But he had something to tell me: The faucets on the farm needed wrapping with duct tape and newspapers so they wouldn't freeze when winter arrived. He didn't learn that by reading a book or by attending a weekend seminar. After nearly nine decades on the farm, he knew when to do things almost instinctively, like a squirrel knows when to gather nuts. And he knew that when the morning fog started hanging low on the ridges of the Coast Range, winter was coming, which meant wrapping the faucets with duct tape and newspapers.

He was a smart man, but not smart in the way the world thinks. Though he attended Linfield College in nearby McMinnville, he never earned a degree, never took an SAT. But he was a master of self-sufficiency. When he needed drawers for bolts and screws, he didn't head for the store; he took tin snips and cut turpentine cans in half. For Christmas gifts, he would make wind chimes for his grandchildren and pocket-size board games for his great-grandchildren.

He knew what was important in life. What mattered, he figured, wasn't making more money, owning more possessions, and becoming more important. What mattered were his fields, his family, and his faith.

There was a naturalness to him—a realness—that's no longer stylish in our dress-for-success world. When he sang "Amazing Grace" on Sunday morning at the tiny Baptist church that he helped found in nearby Carlton, he was inevitably off a few keys. (OK, more than a few keys.) When he dressed up, his tie was inevitably crooked. But that was just Pop. And when you looked down the pew and heard him singing, you knew that all was well with the world.

He wasn't dynamic or dashing; his standard outfit was overalls, a faded jean jacket, and a hat stitched with a logo from a fertilizer company. He often had a toothpick dangling from his mouth.

His eyes always said more than his words. When family members said good-bye after a visit to the farm, his eyes would grow misty.

He was our witness tree, the man who marked who we were as a family, with an inscription buried deep in the wood.

Well-intentioned relatives gave him calculators, instant-load cameras, and the like for years. He was too polite to refuse them, but most such gifts wound up on a shelf somewhere, seldom, if ever, used.

A month before Pop died, a cousin and I were talking about computers. Pop sat there in his chair, the wall clock ticking incessantly in the background. And I wondered: What must he think of this talk about disk drives, megabytes, and parallel ports? This is a man who was 49 years old when the first electric *typewriter* was introduced. A man who lived through the terms of 19 presidents. A man born into a world of horses and buggies, and died as space-shuttle missions were becoming routine.

In the weeks before his death, he gave away many things to relatives: a button hook he had used to fasten his shoes, a driver's license with a June 30, 1937, expiration date—things that made you realize how ill-fit he was for the world of free-ways and fast food. But the greatest gift he gave was simply being Harry "Pop" Youngberg, farmer.

For the seeds he scattered in his lifetime grew much more than just wheat, strawberries, and corn. And in the family he left behind, those seeds promise to bear much fruit, despite the winds of change.

Gram

> As I went by a pitch-pine wood the other day, I saw a few little ones springing up in the pasture from these seeds which had been blown from the wood....What a feeble beginning for so long-lived a tree! By the next year it will be a star of greater magnitude, and in a few years, if not disturbed, those seedlings will alter the face of Nature here.
>
> —*Faith in a Seed* by Henry Thoreau

Officially, Pop's wife was named Louise. But nothing was very official about my wife's grandparents, and nobody in the family ever called her that. They called her by her real name: Gram. And when they referred to the two of them together, they always said "Gram and Pop," never "Pop and Gram."

The latter would be like referring to Jerry and Ben's ice cream or Decker and Black power tools. It was "Gram and Pop," said with the same cadence as "rock 'n' roll," though I can't recall—and frankly, shudder to even imagine—hearing those two phrases spoken together in the same sentence.

Over the decades, "Gram and Pop" became like a family trademarked name, as if it were a single word representing a single entity (which, in some ways, it was). Together they brought up three children, who gave them 11 grandchildren (including my wife), who gave them 19 great-grandchildren.

The two people complemented and completed each other for six decades. They had an uncommon connection with family members, particularly with grandchildren, who would head for the farm whenever given the chance—even as teenagers.

But Gram and Pop were two different people. Gram was one-of-a-kind. I've never known anyone who so profoundly influenced her entire extended family. I've never known anyone as content. And I've never known anyone who could so perfectly cook an over-easy egg.

Her legacy filtered down to generations behind her like morning sunlight through a kitchen window: soft, unassuming, and yet infusing the entire room with a welcome warmth that lasted long into the afternoon. Oswald Chambers asks, "Which are the people who have influenced us most? Not the ones who thought they did, but those who had not the remotest notion that they were influencing us.... We always know when Jesus is at work because He produces in the commonplace something that is inspiring."

That was Gram, her faith at work. She made a conscious decision to live a godly life, but I am not sure she understood how much we all noticed. In the seemingly pedantic ways of life, she offered the profound, and made of the commonplace something inspiring. My wife speaks of cookie-baking sessions or berry-picking expeditions with her grandmother as if the experiences had some near-mystical quality about them, as if there were something truly noble in growing your own popcorn, embroidering a pillowcase, or feeding a threshing crew.

She grew up in McMinnville, Oregon, about 30 miles southwest of Portland. In 1924, she graduated from Linfield College, met Pop, and married him in her family's living room. Later, they had a son—my wife's father—and two daughters.

Gram Youngberg was 4-H, fresh eggs, a cackling little laugh, and hymns about reaping and sowing. She was the smell of autumn apples, homemade bread, and musty books that had survived nearly a century. She was the simple life before it made the cover of *Newsweek,* recycling before it was cool, and a child-lover before it took an entire village to raise one.

Grandchildren, great-grandchildren, nieces, and nephews would stay on The Farm often during the year. Gram had a ball of string in a kitchen drawer that she added to and took from but never replaced; it was just one tied-together piece of salvaged string. She wasted nothing, including time. Or the chance to make a child happy. If grandkids wanted to walk in mud puddles, she would slap plastic bags over their shoes and let 'em wade. She had a "kid drawer" in the kitchen, with little toys that were so old they would become antiques.

On The Farm, the woodshed was not a place where children were taken to be spanked; it was a place where children were allowed to let their imaginations run free, where they played house and pharmacy, using apple crates for the counters, beans for pills, and the "pop balls" from oak trees for money. In some ways, Gram was a child herself. A niece remembers, as a little girl, complaining about having to walk the half mile to get the mail. "Maybe the horses would be more fun," said Gram and, after saddling up, they galloped their horses down the lane.

Gram noticed all the details in life, the nuances that so many of us miss. While canning, when a jar lid made the "pop" noise as it sealed, Gram would tell it, "Thank you." When you told her something of which she knew little, like how a computer could search and replace a misspelled word, she would cock her head just so, and say, "Why, the *idea.*" She was almost birdlike: small and delicate, a woman with soft white skin. Yet this was a woman who would help Pop brand cows. And had a deep faith that callused her to the cold winds of farm life and beyond.

Her brother enlisted in the army during World War I, was sent to France, and never came home; he died on the Western Front. She weathered the Great Depression. She took in her aging mother-in-law and, later, her aging mother. She watched a sister die following childbirth in 1939. When Pop's health declined, she cared for him and helped him die comfortably.

On Memorial Day, she would place flowers at two nearby cemeteries. One grave in particular drew her attention each year; it was that of a single man whom she had known 50 years ago. He had known he was going to die, she said, and was afraid nobody would remember him once he was gone. She promised she wouldn't forget him. So each year, even decades after he had died, she would put flowers on his grave.

She didn't preach God's love; she lived it. At the age when many people are retiring not only from jobs but from service in their church, she was telling flannel-graph stories for the kids in her Sunday school class, even if only two showed up, which was sometimes the case. Even after Pop died in 1985, she volunteered to paint wooden toy trucks that her retirement home donated to needy children at Christmas.

At 19, I entered Gram's life like Thunder, one of Pop's more spirited horses. I attended one of the most liberal universities on the West Coast, was poised to enter the devilish newspaper business, and had hair longer than hers. She was a Baptist; I had been raised in Methodist and Episcopal churches, had made a commitment to Christ as a high school junior, and was leery about denominations, period, believing membership in "the club" often overshadowed the right reason for gathering. But she loved me anyway. In fact, she said she had been praying for me ever since her granddaughter Sally was a little girl; prayed that God would find her a good mate. She saw beyond hair and jobs and colleges to the deeper stuff.

She did not sing louder or pray longer or decipher Scripture better than those around her. What she did was cook meals for the pastor and his wife after church. Make afghans for overseas missionaries. And give away every type of produce that grew in the ground, from apples to zucchini.

Her children don't remember her telling them that she loved them—not uncommon for her generation—but they remember *knowing* she did. They remember feeling the woman's prayers sustain them when times were tough. She was not as visibly emotional as Pop, but she had a way of making you feel important.

Once she sent us a clip of a story in which she thought an author had tried to copy something I had written. "Everyone says it's not as good as our Bob's," she scrawled on the side of it. "I call it a copycat." Among her last words while lying in a hospital bed were, "I'm so proud of my family."

Nothing much changed on The Farm. Furniture did not move. Rooms weren't remodeled. Entertainment centers weren't purchased. Some would see it as drudgery; Gram, I think, saw it as stability, rhythm, rightness. She never owned a dishwasher, and I don't think she ever envied those who did.

Some, I'm sure, would look at her from a distance and label her an oppressed farm wife. But I don't believe Gram ever saw herself as such. In fact, I believe her willingness to "die to self," to allow Christ to live through her, to continually be living out Philippians 2:3,4 and considering others better than herself—I believe that, in essence, *was* her joy.

At Christmas, she would give each grandchild and family a sack of walnuts, popcorn from her garden, and perhaps a 20-dollar bill; the great-grandchildren would get five dollars in silver dollars stuffed in a miniature felt mitten that she had made herself.

My sister-in-law Ann once said that people always left Gram and Pop's farm with more than they came with. It might have been a fresh loaf of bread, garden produce, or cuttings from a houseplant carefully placed in one of Gram's recycled cereal boxes, which she would lay flat and cut an X in to provide a wide base to hold the plant. But it was more than that: In a world of hypocrisy, even within the church, it was an example of someone who not only knew what was important, but lived it. In a world of style, it was 4-foot-8-inches of sheer substance. In a world of power and greed, it was the humility to allow others to shine while she stayed contentedly in the shadows.

That's what we left with. We left with a standard, an inspiration, a reminder of all that we could be. We didn't know it at the time; we thought all we were taking home with us were cukes and bread and bouquets of daffodils. But it was more. We were taking home deeper things that couldn't be consumed and wouldn't wilt.

We were taking home a heritage.

Woman in the Photo

Any tree, especially a sprawling banyan tree or a tall, gracefully spreading oak, creates and sustains its own microclimate. Trees are by their nature gregarious, and the more trees there are, the more pronounced their influence on the environment.

—*Planet Earth: Forest*

"Who's the woman in the photo?"

From time to time, visitors in my office at work will ask the question as they survey my surroundings, including the photograph on the wall of a woman in glasses that look like those squint-eyed tail fins of the '62 Chev my folks once drove. She is middle-aged and is wearing a rally uniform with a big C on the front.

One look at the picture, and I can almost feel the November drizzle on my neck as I awaited my moment of glory. This was it. In a few seconds, the opposing kicker would pummel that pigskin and, as the lone kick returner, I would gather it in my arms as if cradling history itself, dodging, dancing, and twisting up the sidelines while the crowd roared its approval.

This was the start of no ordinary game of football. This was the 1972 Turkey Bowl, an annual gathering of eight teenage souls at Cloverland Park in Corvallis, Oregon. Never mind that such games, at that very moment, were going on all over the country. Never mind that we were a bunch of has-beens and never-would-bes, a motley collection of just-back-from-college boys who, when posing for the annual postgame photo, looked like a blend of loggers, hippies, and the "before" example of a laundry-detergent commercial. Never mind that the "crowd" consisted of five people (down a tad from previous years since our official photographer, my father, hadn't shown up yet).

In my vivid imagination, we were an important part of gridiron history, dating back to the days when nineteenth-century New England boys would spend Thanksgiving Day kicking a blown-up pig's bladder through the streets. We were Jim Thorpe, George Gipp, and the Four Horsemen of Notre Dame. We were Johnny Unitas, Joe Namath, Bart Starr, and Terry Baker, the only player from our hometown university, Oregon State, to ever win a Heisman Trophy. We were the days before artificial turf and domed stadiums and uniforms that never got muddy.

We were suddenly distracted by some commotion on the sideline.

"Hey, Welch, get a load of your mom," said my teammate John "Hands" Woodman.

The words blindsided me like a Dick Butkus blitz. I didn't have time to consider what they might mean. I only knew that at age 18, when you're about to partake in a macho game of mud football, you don't want to hear a teammate say, "Get a load of your mom."

I looked over at the sidelines in much the same way you might look at video footage of a man being gored by a bull on the streets of Pamplona: knowing you wouldn't like what you would see, but knowing you couldn't *not* look. There she stood, my wonderful mother—adorned in her 1942 Corvallis High rally uniform.

What was she, nuts? Why did it have to be *my* mother? Everyone else's mother was home doing what mothers were supposed to be doing on this day: fixing a turkey or ironing a tablecloth or pretending to listen to Uncle Harry's story about passing his kidney stone. But my mother, at age 44, was wearing a pleated skirt and a white turtleneck sweater with a giant C on it. My mother was leading the crowd of five in "sis-boom-bah" cheers that hadn't emanated from a megaphone since the days of Franklin Delano Roosevelt.

The "crowd" loved it. My teammates loved it. My opponents loved it. It was vintage Marolyn, the gregarious free spirit of Norwood Street, the woman who water-skied way beyond the legal age limit, fed sea gulls leftover spaghetti, and, at an Oregon State basketball banquet, hammed it up for a photo with a seven-foot center because she was a gregarious woman and knew her basketball-crazy son would think it was cool.

The "crowd" may have loved it. Nor, honestly, did I hate it. I just didn't want any newcomers to think that the two of us might possibly be related. It was time to get on with the game, I suggested. And in a few moments, the game began. As we played, I pretended not to hear her as she shouted her encouragement from the sideline. The game wore on. My team lost.

In the years to come, we played three more Turkey Bowls, then all but one of us left town to get jobs or hitchhike around the country or go to graduate school or get married and have children. It's been 25 years since that November morning. I am now 44—the same age my mother was on that day she appointed herself the Turkey Bowl yell queen—and the other day, I overheard one of my sons telling a friend I was, well, nuts.

I'm not sure exactly why he told his friend that. Maybe it was because last December, for our church's Christmas program, in front of 500 people at a civic auditorium, I wrapped myself in two 100-bulb strings of blinking Christmas lights, and, extension cord trailing behind, walked onto the blackened stage as the emcee.

Maybe it was because on my son Ryan's sixteenth birthday, when we couldn't get any service at a restaurant, I used my cell phone to politely call the dining-room manager and ask—as I watched her from 30 feet away—if I could please get some menus at Table 23.

Maybe it was because at a huge outdoor Rose Bowl party for the University of Oregon, I wound up holding college classmate and professional golfer Peter Jacobsen's paper-plate lunch so he could be photographed with a friend of mine. And after he left, I instinctively took a picture of his half-eaten chicken. Why? Because I knew my golf-crazy son would think it was cool.

My mother knew then what I know now: The world needs laughter.

I spend much of my workday at a newspaper, editing stories about people and values and choices.

I read stories about parents who neglect their children, parents who abuse their children, at times parents who kill their children.

I help a group of high schoolers write, illustrate, and photograph a youth page each week, and get to know some kids who are starving for approval, for someone to notice them, for someone to tell them they're OK.

I coach kids and have seen fathers who scream at their children, berate their children, or drop off their children and leave to throw darts at a tavern with their girlfriend.

My mother knew then what I know now: Children need to be cheered on from the sidelines.

At the time, I felt embarrassed; in fact, my mom says I once asked her why she couldn't be more like a particular friend's mom, a woman who looked and dressed like Harriet Nelson of "Ozzie & Harriet" TV fame, called her son "Donald" instead of "Don," and would never even *think* of letting us play knee football in the living room like my mom would.

My mother, on the other hand, took a volleyball and net every Wednesday night during the summer and drove an hour into the farmland to help migrant workers have some fun. She often asked me if I wanted to come, but I never said yes. I never saw what she saw.

At 18, your vision is blurred. You don't realize that, right in front of you, you're being offered a gift that lots of kids never get to open. But then you grow up and the scales fall off your eyes, and you realize that your mom wasn't on those sidelines in the rain to call attention to herself or because she was a lush or because she wanted to embarrass you. She was there for one reason and one reason only: because she cared.

Time is a teacher. I heard those cheers, Ma. Every one. I cradle them deep inside and, in small, unseen ways, they helped me grow up feeling safe and significant in a world in which many children did not.

So anyway, that's the long version of the answer to the woman-in-the-photo question. Usually, I give the other version when people ask who it is.

"That," I say with quiet pride, "is my mom."

Sinking Roots

Mr. Kintigh's Christmas Tree

Not until the first true leaves unfurl from the first shoot can the process of photosynthesis begin—and with it, the little tree's internal life-support engine. During this phase of the tree's life, it is particularly vulnerable. Many seedlings cannot sustain leaves, and they quickly die....A few hardy specimens will come through, however.

—Trees of North America

The truckers must have thought the old man was crazy. It was August 1992, and the Columbia Gorge separating Oregon from Washington had become a 150-mile-long heat duct. It was 10 P.M. and still more than 90 degrees outside. And there stood 71-year-old Bob Kintigh, waiting for the truck-stop attendant at Biggs Junction to fill the tank of his Ford station wagon—the Ford station wagon that, perceptive people might have noticed, contained strange cargo for these parts in August: a single Christmas tree.

In a nearly treeless gorge flanked by barren rimrock, the scene was no less a juxtaposition of time, place, and object than a shirtless surfer walking barefoot through a Minnesota snowstorm. But dreamers like Mr. Kintigh fix their eyes on their destinations, not on the doubters. Dreamers press on, their imaginations steeled not on the obstacles in the way, but on how they might be overcome.

In the heat of the August night, he sprayed water on the branches of his Christmas tree. As for the truckers—well, let them laugh, he figured. This trip was not meant to impress anyone around him. It was meant to fulfill a dream he'd had for a long, long time.

He glanced at his watch, paid the attendant, and continued his journey north. As he made his way across the wheat fields of eastern Washington on this August night, he pictured it once more: a tree from Kintigh's Mountain Home Ranch—a tree he had raised himself from a tiny seed—decorated in its Christmas-best and standing proudly in the White House in Washington, DC.

He is a small, strong man, Mr. Kintigh. He is a stocky Sean Connery, his white beard suggesting a gentle blend of Santa Claus and sophistication. He is deeply tanned, a testament to decades of working outdoors. He has thick, stubby hands callused from work as a tree farmer and from other jobs, like tending his hundreds of rhododendrons and mowing the lawn at the nondenominational church he attends.

He loves things that grow. He loves trees. He loves Psalm 1:3, which says that the man who trusts in God "is like a tree planted by streams of water, which yields its fruits in season and whose leaf does not wither. Whatever he does prospers."

His wife, Margaret, meanwhile, is a wise, quiet-spirited woman. In a church growth group to which the Kintighs and I belonged, she would make perhaps only a couple of comments all evening, but they would absolutely burst with wisdom and insight.

Together the two of them raised their five children that way—sunk their children's roots in the fertile soil enriched by the Living Water. Took their children to church. Taught them God's Word. The five had grown to adulthood with the usual bumps and bruises, but had grown straight and true, nonetheless.

When Mr. Kintigh talks about them, it doesn't matter that they are now 50, 48, 46, 41 and 36 years old. They are still his and Margaret's children, and it is not uncommon for his eyes to grow watery as he refers to them. For Mr. Kintigh is a sentimental man, and he has seen some of his children buffeted by the harshest of elements. When that happens to a parent's child, it does not matter whether that child is 46 or 4. You hurt.

❧ ❧ ❧

Born in Pennsylvania, Bob Kintigh always wanted to live out West. "When I was born, my feet were just pointing that way," he says.

He grew up in the rural land east of Pittsburgh, where he helped his father on the farm. He walked in the woods. He read books, particularly science books. He knew by the time he was in eighth grade he wanted to spend his life among the trees. And so he went to Penn State to pursue a forestry degree.

There he met a young botany student named Margaret who had eschewed the more-common home ec or education track for women to study plant pathology and genetics. The two wound up merging their interests, often taking trips to a botanical treasure called Bear Meadows and taking hikes up Mount Nittany.

They graduated and got married. He left on a destroyer to help fight World War II; she went to work at a naval aircraft factory in Philadelphia. At war's end, he returned home, and they headed West. He earned a master's degree in forestry at the University of California at Berkeley. Then the two moved north to Oregon.

Outside of Springfield, in the southern part of the lush Willamette Valley, they bought and began nurturing 170 acres of rolling-hill land that they would call Kintigh's Mountain Home Ranch: a blend of timber, Christmas trees, and nursery stock, all of it so immaculately kept that, from a distance, it looks like part of a Lionel train set.

Bob and Margaret raised trees and reared kids—millions of the former, five of the latter: Dave, Paul, Ann, Mark, and Dan. It was "Bonanza" with a few twists: The family ranch hands trimmed trees instead of branding cattle, and Pa had Ma, who spent much of her time at home with young children.

The children survived the tumultuous sixties; so did the tree farm, which was pummeled by the 1962 Columbus Day storm, buried by record-breaking snow in 1969, and parched by an occasional summer of drought.

The seventies slid by. The Kintigh children grew up and started families of their own, though living on or near the ranch. Soon not only were the Kintigh kids racing in and out of the modest home atop a hill, but so were the Kintigh grandkids. The two youngest sons, Dan and Mark, started learning the business so that someday they could take over for their father.

Mr. Kintigh, meanwhile, became Senator Kintigh—he would serve as a Republican state legislator for 12 years—and continued to hone his skills as a forester.

He experimented with different seeds in different locations on the farm. He did controlled crossbreeding with some of his elite Douglas-fir seed trees, planting two fields with the seedlings grown from this "premium blend." But above all, he came to believe that the most important thing in growing a good tree was this: the care it was given in its early years.

In fact, he came to believe that the time a tree spent in the greenhouse might be more important than the time it spent outside it. In the first few weeks, the seedlings, like a small baby, need nearly constant care; because of their shallow root depth, they need frequent watering. Climatic conditions must be carefully monitored to reduce the possibility of disease; high temperatures can be deadly. As the seedlings grow, they're fertilized to strengthen their roots and nutrient reserve.

Then it's time they're "hardened off"—prepared for planting in the much-tougher world of the forest. Water is reduced. Greenhouse covers are removed to expose the trees to natural winds and the decreasing temperatures of fall. By early winter, they are ready to be on their own and, as Mr. Kintigh says, "they might bend, but they will not break."

And so it is with children. Consider a recent article that ran in *The Register-Guard* newspaper:

> A child commits suicide every four hours
>
> A child is arrested for a drug-related crime every seven minutes.
>
> A baby is born to a teenage mother every minute.
>
> A student drops out of a public school every five seconds during the school day.
>
> After decades of research in childhood development, experts now know with great certainty that those tragic outcomes are often set in motion in the earliest months of life. The lack of certain kinds of input from parents can knock development off course like a rocket misfired at its launch.
>
> "Kids do go into different trajectories, and those trajectories get set early in life," child expert Dr. Neal Halfon said. "We have to help society understand that what happens to a child early in life really determines what happens to them in adulthood."

What happened to Bob and Margaret's children in adulthood is that they all soared boldly into adult airspace—by all accounts, right on course. Then tragedy struck some of them, at times with the heart-sinking suddenness of the Challenger explosion.

First, Dave and his wife Marla's 20-year-old son died in an automobile accident while overseas in the service. Then four years later, cancer struck Marla; she, too, died. Out of the blue, Ann's husband left her. No less suddenly, Mark's wife left him for another man.

I remember the Sunday morning that Mark arrived at church with a look on his face like you would expect from a man who had just survived a jet crash. He mumbled something about needing to talk to someone, then explained to a pastor and me what had happened.

Rare is the family that goes through this much pain in this short a time; rarer still is the family that survives it. It is easy to oversimplify the healing of the human heart; Dave and Ann and Mark will forever carry the scars of the losses they've faced. But though Bob and Margaret's children may have bent, they did not break. They continued to trust God, refusing to let their pain paralyze them for life. They pressed on, their imaginations steeled not on the obstacles in the way, but on how they could be overcome.

Why? In part because Bob and Margaret nurtured them well when they were young, which became a legacy of strength in their children when they weren't so young. Dave has remarried and continues to live just down the road from Bob and Margaret. Ann, after fighting to save her marriage, finally let go; several years later, she married a pastor whose wife had died, and the two of them recently founded a new church together.

Mark has stayed deeply involved in the lives of his children, one of whom was recently named one of our community's students of the month, in part because of a 4.0 GPA.

Mark has refused to slip into the bitterness that many others might have in his situation. When I see him at church, I no longer see a crash victim; I see a survivor. I see one who perseveres. I see him, as I do his siblings, as a noble fir, nurtured decades ago to withstand the winds and droughts of today.

❧ ❧ ❧

After stopping at a motel in Eastern Washington, Mr. Kintigh finally arrived in Spokane, where dozens of growers from around the country had gathered to see who the National Christmas Tree Association judges would choose to supply the White House with its tree. He was confident—his tree had weathered the trip well—but he had been this close twice before, in 1980 and 1988, and had been passed over both times.

Instead of grousing about being overlooked, though, he had learned from those defeats. In 1980, in Illinois, he had learned that judges want a tightly sheared tree, not the kind he had entered. And in 1988, in Maine, he had learned to never send your tree across the country by air freight. Along the way, the tree had been left out in the sun and had had foliage burned, even though it had been wrapped in burlap.

This year, 1992, he had vowed to avoid both mistakes. He had groomed 20 trees from his prized field and personally sheared each one as they grew. Then he chose the best one of the bunch and custom trimmed it more. The late-summer heat had left the soil dry and hard; to reduce stress on the tree, he dug a trench at the drip line and, in the week prior to cutting it, poured 75 gallons of water into the mini-moat.

Because of the heat, he cut the tree late in the afternoon, gently placed it in the station wagon, and began the ten-hour trip to Spokane. He stopped several times to give it water. Though it may have seemed an extreme measure, he knew the competition would be just as diligent. In fact, a grower from North Carolina had gone so far as to not even cut his tree before shipping it. Instead, to keep it as fresh as possible for the judging, he had dug out the tree, root ball and all, and had it sent cross-country in a refrigerated truck.

After an overnight stay in Spokane, Mr. Kintigh pulled his station wagon into the conference center, gently took out his tree, and carried it to the judging area. This was it. He had done all he could do; now, it was up to the judges.

They deliberated for several hours. Finally, the results were announced. Mr. Kintigh scurried to a pay phone and called Margaret. "We won!" he said. "We get to furnish the White House tree. Tell the boys!"

❧ ❧ ❧

In December 1992, Mr. Kintigh went to Washington. So did Margaret, their daughter, two sons, four daughters-in-law, six grandchildren, and an 18½-foot grand fir that a White House representative had flown out and personally chosen from the Kintigh Mountain Home Ranch. (Mark and Dan needed to stay home and handle the Christmas tree operation, which, of course, was in its busiest season.)

The Kintighs were touring the White House when President George Bush and his wife, Barbara, arrived from a Thanksgiving holiday at Camp David.

"Are you the Christmas tree people?" asked the president.

"Yes we are," said Mr. Kintigh.

It was then that Mr. Kintigh realized he wasn't in Kansas anymore; more precisely, he wasn't at a truck stop in Biggs Junction, Oregon, anymore. Instead, he was standing in the same building where U.S. presidents had lived since John Adams became the first president to live there in 1814.

President Bush and Barbara Bush shook hands all around, [illegible] for a photographer, and posed with the entire Kintigh clan. The family toured the grounds, went to a reception in their honor hosted by Mrs. Bush, and saw the Blue Room, where the tree was later placed.

For a family that had been through its share of pain—and would have more to face in the years ahead—it was an event they would never forget. For the man who had grown the tree, it was a reminder to not let go of your dreams. And for me, a casual observer of the folks who live on and around the Kintigh Mountain Home Ranch, it was a reminder that, in the end, it's often the beginning that makes the difference.

Worlds Apart

> Nature did not mean plants to move; roots want to take hold and stay. A seedling undergoing transplant shock is a poignant, desperate sight—every plant part withers and curls; the stem goes limp and lies flat on the ground.
>
> —*Bringing a Garden to Life*

As we enter a new millennium, forecasts of the future abound. In particular, I've been reading recently what the so-called experts believe will become of the family in the twenty-first century. I found it fascinating.

Meanwhile, a friend of mine recently shared with me some portions of a letter she sent her grandchildren about what her life has been like in the past. I found it equally fascinating.

What intrigued me most was how much the culture of family has changed in America—and will probably continue to change—in just one person's lifetime. So realizing that this country's future depends, in part, on what values each of us decides to defend, I offer a contrast of the two points of view: how some people foresee the future and how one simple, yet profound, woman has seen the past.

To some degree, legacies are influenced not only by what [illegible], as individuals, pass on to our children, but by what our [illegible]re passes on to them as well. I'll let you decide which kind of world you'd want your grandchild to inherit as I offer my friend Pat Taylor's remembrances of yesterday, interspersed with the pundits' predictions of tomorrow:

> The first memory I can recall is sitting on a porch swing with a very pretty, tall, straight lady holding me on her lap. I later learned this was my grandmother, who I am told died when I was two years old. She always had on a crisp, starched, white apron and her hair was dark and pulled back in a bun on the back of her head. I can't recall anything she ever said to me, but I can still remember that feeling that her love wrapped me up like a warm blanket.

The family of the twenty-first century, say many experts, won't be the always-cheery Jetsons. Instead, it will be divided by divorce and further muddied by remarriage more so than even today. The number of single parents will increase, as will the number of working moms and out-of-wedlock babies. "Communities either will be segregated into male and female sectors or inhabited entirely by women who have decided they can do without men, with cloning and artificial insemination the primary means of procreation," reports *USA Today* magazine.

> Christmas morning was filled with electric excitement. The first one awake quickly got everyone up and going. There was a rushing of little feet running and tripping over each other down the stairs to the wonder of the Christmas tree. They were enthralled by the lights and smells and packages under the tree. I think right then was when I started realizing what family bonds and love were all about, and felt extremely blessed. It seemed then, and still does, that God sends a wonderful abundance of love to Earth at Christmas time.

Marriage contracts will become common, and many will include escape clauses so people can avoid the dreaded "till-death-do-us-part" stuff. Responsibilities will be blurred, complex, disputed. "After a divorce, is a person still responsible for helping care for relatives from a former spouse's side of the family?" asks *The Futurist* magazine.

> When I was maybe 12, the war was on and both of my brothers were in the army. One was in the South Pacific and the other in Europe. It was a sad time, when almost every week or so you heard of someone who you knew who was either killed or wounded. My mother said we cannot have a Christmas tree when the boys have such a horrible way to live. We were all heavy-hearted. My dad left about noon and when he returned he had a beautiful tree. We were so happy, we danced around the tree and sang songs and decorated for hours.

"The accretion of step-relatives and former in-laws will be legally messy and increasingly bewildering to children, who will have to divide their loyalties and love among stepmothers, birth mothers, biological fathers, and ex-stepparents," reports *Time* magazine in its "Beyond the Year 2000" special edition. The extended family, it says, will be a tangled web of loyalties and obligations. Incest, once considered an absolute taboo, will become less black and white as families bend and blend.

> Our family grew up around the big, old oak dining room table. Everyone gathered there for our evening meal, which we called supper. Papa would always say the blessing, and no one ate a bite until he said "Amen." Then it was everyone on their own. Food was passed and everyone talked at once. My brother Tommy was the comedian and could always turn a dull story into something funny. He would have us laughing until we would cry.

Edward Cornish, president of the World Future Society, foresees a time when America's streets will be akin to Dickens' London—or more like Brazil, where hordes of children wander aimlessly. Schools, which are already having to become replacements for parents in some cases, may become 24-hour havens for children of abuse and neglect.

> In the summertime after dinner, we all moved to the front porch. Mama and Papa sat on the big swing as did all the other neighbors. The kids all gathered in the streets, and the games began. We played red rover, tag, hide and go seek, statues, hop scotch, etc. Everyone was your neighbor and even more like your brother.

More people will work at home. The bad news? Work will also become more international in scope and, thus, will need to be done essentially 24 hours a day. Home life and work life will more easily become blurred, which will make it harder for parents and children to interact.

> There were no motels at this time and so when relatives or friends traveled they were expected to stay at your house overnight. Everyone got a blanket and a pillow, and you found a space of floor and claimed it as your spot. Sometimes when we had family reunions there would be so many cousins and aunts and uncles that people slept under the big oak table and even in the bathtub. There was lots of talking and laughing way into the night before everyone gave up and went to sleep. These are lovely memories I carry into my old age.

The rich will get richer, the poor poorer. "There will be a mass market for luxury goods of all kinds, with incomprehensible prices paid for items in extreme demand because of their prestige value," says *The Futurist*. So much for those who think the best things in life—like relationships—are free.

The family, meanwhile, could turn into something almost unrecognizable. Some will suggest that the government allow families to incorporate as businesses. *Time*, in its special edition, wonders whether the family will exist at all. "Given the propensity for divorce, the growing number of adults who choose to remain single, the declining popularity of having children and the evaporation of time families spend together, another way may eventually evolve," it says. Family-based reproduction might give way to state-sponsored baby hatcheries à la Aldous Huxley's *Brave New World*. Embryos could be brought to infant stage in a lab, not in a womb. In short: designer kids. Nurses, not parents, could feed the children; so, perhaps, could automated machines.

> God has blessed me with many good memories. My greatest blessing in life, though, was when I was 20 and your father was born. I held him and talked of college and all the wonderful things he would do in life. I never doubted his potential, because I always knew God was with him. Besides this blessing, God gave me your mother to love, and guess what followed that? My most beloved grandchildren. You have each made my life full and complete. My heart bursts with the pride and joy I have in each of you.

The Draining of the Red Sea

A tree that has grown up in a particular landscape reveals something essential about the history and character of that place; the place changes the tree, and the tree changes the place.

—*Bringing a Garden to Life*

In the beginning were the words. They came from my then seven-year-old son, Ryan, shattering my Saturday morning slumber with all the subtlety of a low-flying F-15. For parents of small children, they are among the seven most feared words in the English language: "Don't worry, I fixed my own breakfast."

Still in my pajamas, I dragged myself to the scene of the crime. Indeed, my son had fixed his own breakfast—a bowl of Alphabits cereal, which explained why the kitchen floor was strewn with enough letters to spell the entire lineage of David. I sighed. This was going to be an interesting two weeks.

The previous night, my wife, Sally, had left on a short-term missionary trip. Her goal was to bring medicine, encouragement, and the love of Christ to the needy people of Haiti. Mine was less lofty: to have a measurable pulse when she returned.

When it was over, my sons and I had survived, I had a new appreciation for single parents, and we had been part of one of those survival stories that has been told many times since it happened a decade ago. It is a story that will undoubtedly be passed down from generation to generation, each telling of the story infused with just a bit more drama so that by the time it gets to my great-great-granddaughters and grandsons, it will be the suburban equivalent of the Donner Party crossing the Sierra Nevadas.

Except we weren't trying to really get anywhere, except off to school and work each day—and back.

As a single parent, the first thing I learned was that if you don't do something, it ain't gonna get done. And if by some small miracle it does get done, it ain't gonna get done right—at least in my case. Before Sally left, I just assumed that whenever you ran out of soap, the Soap Fairy magically replenished the dish. I also imagined the Soap Fairy had relatives: the Milk Fairy, the Dental Floss Fairy, and the Light Bulb Fairy, among others. What I learned is that the only things in a household that magically replenish themselves are soiled laundry, dirty dishes, and junk mail.

I now understand why God said it is not good for a man to be alone. He knew what we needed: a helpmate who knows instinctively how to remove strawberry Jell-O stains from a white pet rabbit. (Don't ask.) One who also knows that you can't make whipped cream out of half-and-half ("Why won't this blasted stuff get foamy?"), and that certain antistatic thingamajigs go in the dryer along with the clothes. (I learned the latter after noticing my four-year-old son, Jason, walking around with something clinging to the back of his sweatshirt: a pair of static-laden Batman undershorts.)

With my wife gone, time seemed to stand still. "Dad," reminded Jason, "you have to remember to wind the clocks. Mom does."

I pressed three dress shirts before realizing the iron wasn't plugged in. I let so much toothpaste build up in the kids' sink that I could have chipped it off and had a week's supply of breath mints. On one short trip we took, I packed two right-footed boots—and no left—for my oldest son. And somehow I wound up the two weeks with nine widowed socks. Nine!

But socks weren't the only things that got lost—so did my time with the kids, and, at times, my patience. I discovered that houseplants left unattended don't thrive. And neither do children, who need emotional watering to flourish.

Too often, I would plunk the kids in front of a Disney video so I could do more important things, like scrape last night's lasagna from the dining-room table or embark on a search-and-destroy mission for moldy food in the fridge.

I got grumpy. Early on, I kept my cool. When Ryan locked half the neighborhood kids in a pup tent (yes, it is possible to get *locked* inside a pup tent), I handled the episode without even raising my voice. But when he used a fork to catapult lima beans at his brother across the table, I became Mike Dikta after a last-second loss.

An uneasy truce ensued, but on Day 12 (after forgetting to give Ryan his lunch money for the second day in a row), I sensed a loss of confidence in Dad. The clue was Ryan saying, "I want Mom back," and Jason adding: "Me, too. Right *now*."

It was time to play my trump card. The kids wanted to paint their wooden sailboats, so I obliged. I made sure the paint was water-soluble. After what I had been through, the last thing I needed was a set of permanently stained shirts.

How was I to know that my sons were planning to launch their freshly painted boats in the bathtub? "Dad, all the paint washed off," said Jason, sitting in a tub of what looked to be tomato juice.

I drained the Red Sea. While putting my now-red kids to bed, the phone rang. Happily, I thought that perhaps things in Haiti had gone so smoothly that my wife's missionary team was coming home a day early. Not quite. But for a limited time only, I could have my drapes dry-cleaned for a special low, low price.

"Uh, thanks, but—"

The buzzer sounded from the basement. My wash load was lopsided again.

"Dad, you forgot to go over my spelling words with me," Ryan yelled from his bunk.

That's when the pet rabbit knocked over the wooden Noah's ark puzzle, scattering elephants, zebras, and giraffes across the living-room rug, two-by-two.

OK, so we didn't come through this ordeal unscathed. Still, somehow it challenged us, changed us, molded us. It drew us closer together. Despite their "we want Mom" demands at the dinner table, the boys later admitted I had done, in their words, "OK," which I take as high praise. And I felt like it helped send our intergenerational roots just a little bit deeper.

All said, more than ten years later I'm still haunted by those questions that, I suppose, haunt all survivors, and may haunt generations of Welches to come.

Chief among them: Just where *do* those missing socks go?

Strangers and Pilgrims

> Another type of pruning is called training. The object in training is to help the young tree develop a strong branch structure. Properly trained trees will require little corrective pruning as they mature.
>
> —*The Simple Act of Planting a Tree*

A hint of daylight lightens the sky, distinguishing, for the first time, the Cascade Mountains to the east and the Coast Range to the west. It is just after 5 A.M., and a summer day has begun on a Mennonite dairy farm in Oregon's Willamette Valley. The Mennonites are shirtsleeve relatives of the horse-and-buggy Amish of Lancaster County, Pennsylvania, and work is to their lives what wool is to yarn.

Three teenage girls don't cherish the sound of a 5 A.M. alarm on milking days. But while their father cleans manure from the barn with his tractor, his daughters attach the cows to the milking machines. The girls wear rubber boots, pastel dresses, sweatshirts, and prayer caps, the latter covered with bandannas.

There is little talk, little action, little sound—nothing but the *click-pfffft-click-pfffft* drone of the milking machine. Then, seemingly out of nowhere, the girls break into song, harmonizing words to a Mennonite hymn that the world will never hear:

> The music of heaven is sweeter in measure
> And purer in every strain
> Than the music of Earth, so it fills us with pleasure
> As it thrillingly rolls over valley and plain.

Along with a newspaper photographer, I spent six months, off and on, researching a story on the Mennonites who live in the rural lands north of my home in Eugene. Around here, they are the ultimate nonconformists: people who live without television, radios, stereos, and musical instruments. People who have never voted, watched a movie, seen a football game, bought insurance, sat in a courtroom, rolled a bowling ball, served in the military, or worn a ring. People who, in some cases, have never even heard of an Oreo cookie.

I came away from the experience inspired in many ways about these self-described "strangers and pilgrims." Their lives imbue great respect for God, family, tradition, discipline, responsibility, simplicity, humility, and heritage. I don't endorse all that Mennonites believe and do, but I exalt their emphasis on teaching and modeling to their children—passing on the values rooted in the Reformation of sixteenth-century Europe.

At mealtime, all nine children bow their heads for prayer, which is followed by a hymn sung in homespun harmony. At the private school all the Mennonites attend, eyes rivet on the teacher and nary a whisper is heard—a far cry from my sons' public-school experience. At graduation, students file into the gym—boys in one line, girls in another—with the precision of the Blue Angels. At home, children do chores—from picking fruit to making meals to shoveling manure—with a quiet determination that belies their ages.

Even when the father and his nine-year-old son make a milk delivery into Eugene, I notice no loosening of morals and composure. At one store, a back-room employee scolds Roy, as if he were a child, for taking empty crates without checking with her. The son watches, wondering how his father will respond. Instead of lashing back with a verbal counterattack, the father says nothing in return, just goes about his business.

The Mennonites live with purpose, with structure, with a belief that the two go together. At church, when it's time to pray, they fall to their knees, turn and bow their heads in the pew, all with the urgency of a sixties air-raid drill.

People, not materialism, matter in this neck of the woods. When a young couple had a baby, three women from the church showed up and canned more than 100 quarts of strawberry jam for the family one morning. And two years later, when the little girl was diagnosed with cystic fibrosis, the small church took up an offering—enough to cover the baby's $274-a-month pharmacy bill for an entire year.

There is a cost to all of this. A young man who came from outside the Mennonite circle talked of how, in his father's eyes, he had failed. The man wanted his son to get a doctorate degree, get tenure at the university where he taught writing, build security, live the American Dream. Said the young man: "God's Word doesn't say anything about an obligation to get a Ph.D. But it does say something about having responsibility to raise my children in the nurture and admonition of the Lord. I can't do that if I'm stuck off in some room, writing a paper so I can get a degree."

The Mennonites' paint-by-numbers existence leaves little room for artistic flair, but it also leaves little room for error. Suicide is rare, therapy bills nonexistent, crime rates low. The Mennonites worry about keeping gum, not guns, out of school. True, some extreme cases exist. But usually when a teenager rebels, it's not apt to mean he's joined a gang, but that, late at night, when everyone's asleep, he's listening to country-western music on his borrowed radio.

In a sense, conservative Mennonites live like all people live—by making trade-offs. They give up one thing in order to get another. Little opportunity exists for Mennonites to change the system, to air points of view, to ask questions. Roles are played from unalterable scripts. Right and wrong are seared into this micro-society, tempered by time and tradition. But if such rigidity has its cost, it pays dividends as well. For the Mennonites believe that in forgoing certain freedoms, they avoid certain snares.

The Mennonites forgo entertainment, yet preserve innocence; if no TV means missing some educational and entertaining shows, it also means missing the 18,000 murders the average American teenager will see in his or her youth, and teen-aimed shows such as "Dawson Creek," one of which recently featured teacher-student sex.

They frown on freedom of expression, but experience little social pressure to outdo one another; children don't plead for the latest fashion. Men don't trample each other for job promotions.

They don't reach for the stars, but neither do they reel with shattered illusions. Life, they believe, was meant to be lived with one's sleeves rolled up and head bowed, not chasing the wind.

For all that they give up, the Mennonites' willingness to promote a heritage handed down generation after generation gives them a sense of stability, community, and connectedness. Nearly all children grow up with a father and mother in the home; divorce is virtually nonexistent. Seldom do families move or change jobs. If Mennonites go through mid-life crises, they are well-hidden crises. Children are raised realizing they're part of something old and revered.

In my office at work, which often resembles an air-traffic control tower for feature stories that are taking off, landing, and (sometimes) crashing in flames, I sometimes lean back in my chair and look at a photograph given to me by the photographer who worked on the Mennonite project with me.

It is of a little girl in a cotton dress. Pigtails flying, she is running on a makeshift dock that juts into a farm pond. It is a scene reminiscent of another era and brings to mind something mentioned by one of the mothers. "My daughters," she said, "are being raised the same way I was raised."

In a king-of-the-hill culture in which not even the kings seem fulfilled, a mall-mad culture in which consuming seems to have become our reason for living, who can argue with that?

Out of Thin Soil

Timberline designates the limit of forest either high up on mountainsides, in frigid polar regions, or adjacent to grasslands. It is composed of a number of tree species, each having distinctive adaptations which allow it to endure in a harsh environment.

—*Timberline: Mountain and Arctic Forest Frontiers*

Oscar Hernandez grew up in a large cardboard box in El Salvador. He did not worry about whether he had the right kind of Nikes on the first day of school or whether he would get the same lunch period as his friends. Instead, he worried about going to sleep at night and not waking up, about being killed by government soldiers while he slept, as had happened to some of his friends.

He was the oldest of seven children. He never knew his father. He never knew a childhood. He never knew a dream.

In 1991, I met him when I was assigned to do a newspaper story on a hole-in-the-wall grocery store in Eugene called La Tienditas. Oscar, 32 at the time, owned the store. He was proud of that. In broken English that was far better than my broken Spanish, he went on and on about what was in the store, about his customers, about his products.

Midway through the interview, I realized something: This was not a story about a grocery store. It was a story about a person. A journey. A story about someone going from nowhere to somewhere.

That "somewhere" was not Hollywood, Washington, DC, or the moon. It was a tiny store in Eugene, Oregon, whose entire area had less square footage than Safeway's cereal aisle. But in my mind, Oscar Hernandez had traveled a more impressive journey than movie stars, presidents, and astronauts.

"Don't you see?" I said to Oscar. "I don't want to write about your store; I want to write about you. You're the story. You and how you got here."

Oscar did not see. He did not see the heroics I saw. He did not see the courage I saw. In fact, he kept insisting that the store be the focus of the story.

"Don't you see the odds you overcame to get where you are?" I asked.

He honestly didn't. Not at first. But slowly, as we talked about his journey from a cardboard box to owning a grocery store in a city of 135,000 people, he grew to understand.

As his story unfolded, I learned that Oscar got to where he is now not only because of his own stubborn will, but because of others who believed in him, too. In El Salvador, a wealthy philanthropist who employed his uncle as a bodyguard made a deal with the then-teenage Oscar: He would send Oscar to a Jesuit college for a year if Oscar would consistently bring the man notes from the classes, proof that he was attending classes.

"I was exposed to new ideas," Oscar remembers. "I saw the other side, the possibilities."

He moved to Los Angeles, where he continued to make "distinctive adaptations," if you will. He washed dishes at a pizza parlor—an hour one-way trip by bus—to support his family. Later, he picked oranges for $2.40 an hour and lived in a migrant camp.

Someone else believed in him and helped him connect with the University of Oregon, which had a program designed for low-income minorities like himself. Years later, after coming north and attending the University of Oregon, he hatched his dream for a grocery store. Six banks turned him down for loans. People told him he was crazy. When attending a community college to study business, he was told a store like his couldn't cut it in this market.

But he wouldn't give up. In a sense, Oscar reminds me of the pines that grow around some of the rocky rims of Oregon's high-mountain lakes, some not far below the timberline. That they've survived in this harsh environment seems uncanny. That some have actually *thrived* seems almost a miracle, as if they willed their roots to find a toehold in the parched soil wedged between the rocks. They are not the delicate dogwoods that, say, color Augusta National Golf Course. Instead, they are gnarled pines whose beauty and glory lie in their context—trees who made much with what little they had.

It has been almost eight years since I did that story on Oscar Hernandez. He no longer owns that little store. No, he outgrew that space years ago so he moved the entire operation across the street, quadrupled the size, and added a restaurant that many say serves the best Mexican food in town.

He got married and now has two daughters, four and six—children who go to sleep at night and feel safe. Children with childhoods. Children with dreams and possibilities.

I saw Oscar a couple of months ago. I contracted with him to have his restaurant host a banquet for a team of teenage journalists whom I mentor at the newspaper where I work. We had agreed on a fixed price for the event, but when the bill came it was for 70 dollars less than I had agreed to pay.

"Let me pay you what we agreed on," I said.

"No," said Oscar. "You are my friend."

Friend or not, he deserved what we agreed on. I insisted. He insisted otherwise. We argued good-naturedly for a few minutes, but he would not change his mind. I shook his hand and said good-bye, vowing to overpay him by 70 dollars the next year.

Later, I thought of what a strong, giving man he had become, and how I would always remember him not for his store, but for his coming from nowhere to somewhere, then turning and reaching a hand down to his children, so they might get there, too.

Some of the most honorable among us live in the shadows. Such is the case with Oscar Hernandez, a man who has done something much more difficult than most of us will ever do. He didn't continue a legacy. He started one from scratch.

Love Letters

> The trunk and limbs of a living tree are marvels of structural soundness, capable of sustaining a tree hundreds of feet tall through centuries of storms. But they also provide an intricate circulatory system that links the interdependent parts of the tree, supplying every one of its billions of living cells with water and minerals.
>
> —*Forest*

Near as anyone can tell, Sally's grandmother never touched a computer keyboard. She didn't particularly like talking on the phone. Instead, she communicated with her extended family through something far superior to anything high technology could offer, something better than even e-mail.

She reached out and touched us with g-mail—Gram Mail.

Gram Youngberg, who died in the fall of 1997 at the age of 95, wrote letters. Thousands of letters spanning decades and decades, many of which my wife has saved. Part of Gram's legacy was how she lived her life, but part of it, too, was the words she left with us all—words that became an extension of the woman who penned them. Words that helped sustain and link the interdependent parts of her legacy tree.

They tell us of a simple, salt-of-the-earth woman who noticed the daily comings and goings of people with detailed enthusiasm. Like Emily, the young girl in *Our Town* who wonders if anyone but the "saints and poets" really notice the nuances of life around them, Gram, too, noticed the "clocks ticking, and Mama's sunflowers and new-ironed dresses and hot baths...." Mainly, she noticed her extended family and friends.

"Bud Payne," she wrote in one letter, "is still housebound with his severed knee ligament....Max Coffey plans on going to Haiti as a mechanic on the medical team the last of November....My, but Brad and Paul have grown!..."

The letters tell of someone for whom people were the utmost priority. She always wrote more about others than herself. She gloried in her family's victories, commiserated in our defeats. She welcomed in-laws into the family as if we were long-lost friends who, despite no blood links, belonged. She was always more amazed at the accomplishments of others than of her own, though she had many.

"Sally: We are so proud of you and Ann for doing your bit for others in Haiti....

"Today, I've been painting the little wooden fire trucks, 11 of them, for needy children. Then sand them and paint again. Takes almost 20 minutes to do one."

The letters tell of someone who had a special heart for children.

"I'm enjoying my Sunday School class. I have eight 5-6-year-olds and they are nice little kids.

"Your boys' drawings are something. Ryan's cows are an active, happy bunch, and show such action."

The letters tell of someone who reveled in the bounty of God's earth, in weather and soil and seasons and sunsets. "I'm busy with Indian summer crops," she wrote. "I love this time of year. Freezing corn, drying prunes, and finishing up on canning. The apple crop—pears also—were nothing and the few on the trees were wormy and scaly. But there are peaches. And how we enjoyed them!"

In another letter: "Thermometer showed 20 degrees and white frost. Snow in the hills but not here—yet." And still another: "Have you been seeing the glorious sunsets: one last night—and then sunsets during the week. They are gorgeous to behold—to appreciate the handwork of the Lord."

Her letters were full of recipes and news of chickens and cows and gophers and sewing and church potlucks and, of course, Pop. She always took time to ask about how your family was doing. She was fond of exclamation points and, for rare occasions (like when noting a granddaughter's husband was home from the service), used happy faces.

She seldom complained. Oh, a few letters included touching lines in the years after Pop died; she was lonely. But for the most part, she had an uncanny ability to see silver linings in the darkest of clouds, to accept that pain and loss were part of life, much as drought and hail were part of farming.

"Pop is tired," she once wrote, "but we can't complain."

From another letter, extolling the accomplishments of other family members: "Aren't we *lucky*."

Were Gram alive today, I know how she would respond to such glowing accounts of her life. She would react the same way she reacted after I told her what an inspiration she was and that I felt fortunate to be part of her family, even as an adjunct.

"Thanks for the complimentary letter, Bob, but to be honest, I'm very undeserving of such noble motives. For I'm doing what comes naturally. In my growing-up years, I learned to make do, to make use of what is on hand, so I do it."

Decades of letters. Letters whose stamps, in just the last 25 years, went from 8 cents to 32 cents. Letters that, for a while, after Gram broke her arm, were written left-handed. Letters first signed "Gram and Pop" then just "Gram," then finally stopped coming altogether—but only when she physically could no longer write.

Letters reminding us that, over the years, Gram really had two gardens: one with carrots and peas and tomatoes and corn. And one with a son and two daughters and grandchildren and great-grandchildren and nieces and nephews.

In addressing the church at Corinth, Paul writes, "You yourselves are our letter, written on our hearts, known and read by everybody." In a sense, Gram's life was one long love letter to her family and friends and God. A 95-year-long letter.

Nothing would make her prouder than to know that we had tucked that letter in our wallets and purses—better yet, hidden it in our hearts—and lived the same kind of other-oriented life she had lived. She would want us to look for the best in one another. To "make do" with what circumstances we've been given. And, of course, to stop and look at the sunrises and sunsets, for, as she wrote, "They are gorgeous to behold...the handwork of the Lord."

Branching Out

The Handoff

Nothing alive is static. Plants may not be able to walk, but they are changing all the time, as are we.

—*Our Gardens Ourselves*

It hangs proudly (well, in a pathetic sort of way) on the wall at the bottom of the stairs to our ultra-unfinished basement—a place where nobody goes unless he or she is lost or, worse, changing the cats' litter boxes. It is a two-foot by three-foot rectangular piece of warped metal. It is rusted. Once a vibrant green with a red plastic rim, it is now a dingy green with encroaching mold.

Masking-tape lines run across the rectangular object, some of them peeling like badly blistered exterior paint on an aging house. An electric cord dangles from one corner. In the dim light of this staircase nook, you can barely make out the words "Tudor Tru-Action"—in the same way, I suppose, that you might barely make out the word "Titanic" if your submersible were approaching the remains of that once-proud piece of history.

It is the electric football game that I got for Christmas when I was a boy and played year after wondrous year. When talking to elementary-school children about writing, I take it along—at first, hiding it in a pillowcase—because I'm convinced it's what led to my being a writer.

Lately, I've been thinking about the Tudor Tru-Action Electric Football Game more often than usual because my youngest son, now 16, has an electric football game so unlike mine that it is mind-boggling. His is a computer game, and comparing it to mine is like comparing a Maseratti to a Model-T. But comparing the two has also taught me an important lesson: Legacies can transcend technology. And for a guy who carries around a rusty football game in a flowered pillowcase, that can be comforting.

I found it under the Christmas tree when I was about ten, a gift from my parents, and seemingly played it year after year until one day my mother yelled down to me that it was time to go—school was starting and, in college, they don't tolerate missed classes.

For those unfamiliar with electric football, it was played by 22 two-inch-high plastic players permanently frozen in the stiff-arm position. They were motivated not by fiery coaches or seven-digit contracts, but by good vibrations. You lined up the plastic players in offensive and defensive formations—a time-consuming task akin to building the Brooklyn Bridge out of dominoes—and stuck a felt "football" in the arm of the ball carrier. Then you flipped a switch and the players vibrated their way around the metal field in a frenzied funk.

None of the players went where they were supposed to. The ballcarrier would accidentally bounce into his left guard, get spun around, and head 70 yards for a touchdown—in the wrong end zone. Once there, he would vibrate helplessly against the metal wall surrounding the field, totally embarrassing himself and the team.

The quarterback had a spring-loaded arm that allowed him to catapult passes, most of which not only went far over the head of their intended receiver, but landed in the far reaches of the stadium parking lot or under my bed. Any reception was dumb luck, any touchdown a total accident.

I loved it. I played the game hour after hour, day after day, setting up plays and flipping the switch. Bzzzzzzzzzzz. Set up. Bzzzzzzzzzzzzz. Set up. Bzzzzzzzzzzzzz. It nearly drove my mother crazy.

I would play it far into the night, until she would stick her head in my room and say, "Bob, time for bed."

Alas, one day I came home from school, set up the formations, flipped the switch and—click—nothing. I tried it again. Click—nothing. The game had broken. I was crushed, my mother secretly elated. "That thing," she told me years later, "sounded like a high-speed drill."

Suddenly, my life was empty. But out of hollowness came hope. One day I took the offensive players in one hand, the defensive players in the other hand and, almost out of frustration, smashed them together.

Then it dawned on me: Who needed electricity? I designated a ballcarrier and a defense and smashed them together. Why, of course! I could improvise. I didn't need electricity to power this game. I could power it with something far better: imagination.

In my best nasal voice, I became Lindsey Nelson, my favorite TV football announcer, and began offering play-by-play descriptions of the action. I stacked encyclopedias around the field to simulate grandstands— "Section M, right this way"—and used a desk lamp to play night games.

With color crayons, I shaded the end zones to look like the white checkerboard ones at Oregon State, the college in my hometown. With model paint, I outfitted my team in new orange-and-black uniforms, far classier than the all-yellow and all-red teams that had come with the set.

My mother, thrilled that I had created bzzzz-less fun, contributed a 78 rpm record album of college fight songs that I played to add to the pregame excitement. My father made me a set of coat-hanger goalposts, complete with electrical-tape padding around the bases to protect the wayward ballcarriers, of which there were many.

But I didn't stop there. Given that these were the days before domed stadiums and artificial turf, I needed grime. So I brought in mud from Mom's garden. And the ultimate touch, reserved for special occasions, was snow, though the unimaginative may have thought it to be Ivory Soap flakes.

(The players learned to play in the snow. What they never got used to was being sneezed on because I was allergic to the snow; for years, the players' union threatened to strike if pelted by one more mucus storm. Disgusted with such whining, I bagged professional football and decided to stick to an all-college format, where players still played for the sheer love of the game, not mammoth $50,000 contracts with spray-free clauses.)

Snow, rain, sleet, wind, or other stuff—it didn't matter; Oregon State won game after game regardless of the elements. Oh, occasionally when my conscience got to me or I heard grumblings from opposing fans that I wasn't "objective" in my masterminding of the game, I allowed my beloved Beavers to lose a game here or there, though never to their hated rivals to the south, the University of Oregon. But near as I can remember, from the mid-1960s to 1970, Oregon State University went to the Rose Bowl 456 times and won every single time, usually on a last-second pass with no time left on the clock by a quarterback falling backward in his own end zone with three linemen hanging on him.

When a game was over, I would create my own newspaper sports page, complete with story, hand-drawn "photos," and statistics, which included three categories: running yards, passing yards, and total yards. I always thought my drawings were outstanding, as if believing that were Michelangelo still alive, he would bid to replicate them on the ceiling of some domed stadium. But my mother, who was thoughtful enough to save the game instead of trashing it once I grew up, wounded me deeply a few years ago when she said she could never understand why I always drew the players' noses so large.

"Mom," I said, "those were their *face masks*."

"Oh."

Anyway, I tell the elementary-school children, this is what whet my interest for reporting: After each game, I would sit down and, using an old Smith-Corona typewriter, tell the story about what had happened.

Week after week, season after season, I kept playing—even as my collection of players diminished from 22 to 9, thanks to our cocker spaniel Jet, who would eat anything, and my mother's vacuum cleaner, which had a similar appetite. (We'll never know how many players wound up in Mom's Hoover Hall of Fame.)

But those players who survived cleaning day and the cocker spaniel were a gutsy bunch. Talk about playing hurt: Some were missing body parts. Old-timers like to brag about the days of *real football,* when guys played without helmets. That's nothing. I had guys who played without *heads*—and two of them made All-American.

Still, all good things must pass and so did my infatuation with Tudor Tru-Action Electric Football. At 18, I left home. Went off to college; in fact, went to Oregon State University's hated rival to the south, the University of Oregon, because of its journalism program. Got married. Had a son. Had another son.

I never once sat them down and said: Hey, you should be like your old man when he was a kid and find a football game to play at home. Which I find strange since, even as I type these words, Jason is sitting across the room playing computer football with the intensity of Bobby Bowden coaching against University of Florida.

Jason does not *think* he is the coach of a computer football team; he *believes* it. He puts on headphones and school colors. Tonight at a restaurant we found him sketching plays on his napkin.

For those unfamiliar with computer football, it is slightly different from the Tudor Tru-Action Electric Football Game. I had 22 plastic clones; Jason can call up any of more than 100 entire college football *teams*, each of the players having different abilities.

He uses a joystick to control his players, who seem to mind a whole lot better than mine did. Nobody ever runs backwards in computer football. Instead, they score touchdowns and (at least in his pro game) spike the ball, do a dance—some even kneel and pray.

It used to take me about three or four minutes to position all the players to run one play; it takes Jason about ten seconds to choose a play.

He doesn't need to put on a 78 rpm record for his fight songs; when a player scores a touchdown, the computer automatically plays a few bars of the player's school fight song. The computer also makes the crowd cheer, the pads pop, the players grunt, and the official's whistle blow.

Jason doesn't need to use encyclopedias to create make-believe grandstands; he can play his games in any of more than 100 college stadiums that are so real you almost think you're there.

He doesn't need a desk lamp to create night games, his Mom's garden to create mud, or Ivory Soap to create snow. He can create all that with clicks on a computer menu. He doesn't need to do his own play-by-play commentary; a built-in announcer calls the action. Besides, Jason has other things to be concerned about: like which of the hundreds of instant-replay angles he wants to use.

Jason doesn't have to worry about dogs eating his players or his mom's vacuum cleaner thinning his lineup. Then again, he is quick to remind me about the time I exited his football program to use the computer for something else, and in so doing, somehow wiped out an entire football season.

After each game, the computer kicks out complete team and individual stats in dozens of categories, conference standings, even national rankings. Then Jason does something else that I've never once suggested he do: He creates his own newspaper sports page, complete with story, photos, and statistics. But it's a little more sophisticated than my effort, particularly the photos; he can capture individual shots of the best plays and electronically transfer them to his newspaper. Sometimes, for big games, he goes upstairs and interviews himself on videotape.

From there, you would think he would relax. Oh, no. He surfs the web, downloading video plays; scouts other teams; and adds to his personal playbook, which is an inch thick and is packed with more than 250 offensive plays he's designed.

Of course, he can't smell the mud like I could. He can't create the poignant drama that I could when one of my headless linebackers made a game-saving tackle. And when he grows up, he won't be able to pop his game into a flowered pillowcase to show the kids at school.

But as different as electric football and computer football are—as different as 1998 is from 1968—my son and I are still linked by the imagination to dreams, our love of a game, and a desire to tell stories. In that sense, legacies can remain for us a still point in a changing world.

Our legacies to our children can be profound or trivial; this one, on its face, would seem to lean toward the latter. But who knows where those legacies might lead? When I was ten, my parents gave me a simple game that helped draw out some creativity deep within. It sparked an interest in writing. And that interest in writing led to a career that's helped me provide for a family, write four books, and even touch some people's lives.

Somehow, unintentionally, I've handed off this football fantasy to Jason. One day, he may look back at his game-playing and realize it was nothing more than that—just a game. Then again, it may be a seed for something more. So we should never underestimate what we pass on to our children, at times without even knowing it.

Sometimes when I go down the steps to our basement, I see the old Tudor Tru-Action electric football set hanging on the wall, a mere shadow of what it once was, like the skeleton of the great fish at the end of Hemingway's *The Old Man and the Sea*. And I smile inside, remembering the good times the two of us had.

And sometimes when I hear Jason encouraging one of his digitized players to score, or offering imaginary high fives when the player does, or falling onto the floor as if he's just been pelted by a barrel of Gatorade, I smile inside, too, reminded of the good times he's having.

Our worlds are so different and yet not different at all. Last night, while reading in bed, I heard a "touchdown scream" well after midnight. I walked down the hallway and stuck my head in the computer room.

"Coach," I said, "time for bed."

Nickel on the Windowsill

> Let the owner neglect for a while his prized and valued acres, and they will revert again to the wild and be swallowed up by the jungle or the wasteland. The bias of nature is toward the wilderness, never toward the fruitful field.
>
> —*Root of the Righteous*

Life is uncertain. On May 21, 1998, I walked into the lobby at *The Register-Guard* newspaper, where I'm the features editor of Oregon's second-largest paper. It was moments after 8 A.M. Briefcase in hand, I was headed for the staircase when the woman at the main switchboard suddenly hailed me.

"Bob," she said with uncommon urgency in her voice, "there's a student from Thurston High on the phone. Says there's been some kind of shooting. Nobody's in the newsroom yet. Can you take it?"

Surprisingly calm, the young man on the other end of the line told me he was holed up in the yearbook room at the school, about five miles from the newspaper office, in Springfield. Shots had been fired. Students were being confined to classrooms. Rumors were flying that people had been wounded.

"Can you give me the phone number of where you're calling from?" I asked.

He did. I scrawled it and other notes on a piece of scratch paper, took the steps to the upper floor two at a time, and scrambled to find our managing editor's home phone number; the incident, I figured, probably wasn't as serious as the young man had suggested, but you never know. I called the managing editor. I called our photo editor. I told two reporters who arrived just after I did what had happened.

Meanwhile, the newsroom's police scanner squawked with new information. "Suspect in custody," issued a gravelly voice.

Emergency rooms at two hospitals were awaiting victims, a dispatcher said. I started realizing the incident may actually be *more* serious than I had originally thought. Indeed, as the morning unfolded, the story developed like some sort of mutating monster, growing larger and uglier with the arrival of each bit of new information.

By noon, the reality was this: Just before 8 A.M., a young gunman had opened fire on students in the school cafeteria. Two students were dead and 24 were wounded. Back at the suspect's house, two adults, presumably his parents, were dead. The suspect, a 15-year-old freshman at the school, was in custody after students wrestled him to the ground and subdued him.

Within an hour, Springfield, a community of about 50,000 people just east of Eugene, was on radios and TVs around the country. Representatives from *Time* and other magazines were on the phone, negotiating with one of our editors for use of photos we had taken. The national media was descending like locusts in tailored suits and tans way too deep for Oregon in May.

Meanwhile, beyond the network TV trucks that sprang up on the street in front of the high school, the story played out on a much more personal level in the Eugene-Springfield area. One of the victims in critical condition, I learned, was a baby-sitter for a friend at church. Another wounded student was the son of a close friend's teaching partner.

Days later, as my wife and I walked along a chain-link fence in front of the high school that had been covered with flowers, stuffed animals, and words of encouragement, a thought about my son Jason jolted me. When we had first moved to the Eugene-Springfield area, we had rented a house in the Thurston district, across the road from the McKenzie River; in fact, warmed by the bucolic feel of the area's rural outskirts, we had tried for months to find a place to buy in the relatively undeveloped areas north or east of Thurston High. Unable to match desire and price, we had found a home in Eugene.

"Do you realize that if we had stayed in that area, Jason would have been a freshman at Thurston?" I told Sally. "He may have been in that cafeteria."

In the days and weeks to come, thousands of questions would be asked about the incident. But by far the most oft-asked question was simply, *Why?* Why had it happened?

It is a question being asked more frequently these days as teenage violence increases across the country.

The theories—and blame—spread like one of Oregon's grass-seed fields ablaze after harvest. The suspect had been expelled the day before for bringing a weapon to school; the juvenile center should not have released him so soon. The school should have had security guards, said other people.

Antigun activists said the incident was just another tragic reminder of the need for tighter weapon regulations. Others pointed to the media; when television, movies, and video games cheapen life with gratuitous violence, what do you expect from those who absorb that violence? Why did the father buy his son a gun? Why hadn't the state appropriated more money for counseling troubled kids? Why hadn't the school installed a metal detector to prevent weapons from getting on campus? Why hadn't anyone seen this coming?

Though appropriate, the questions represented a wide-angle focus on what, I think, cried out for a close-up lens. In the end, a human being with no immediate provocation aimed a rifle at human targets and repeatedly pulled the trigger. Given a night to think it over, he went out the next morning and did the same thing. Thus, the more potentially telling questions would seem to be:

In the moment he decided to shoot the students, where was the voice of conscience that was supposed to have said: *Don't. This is wrong. People are important. Life is precious. It is wrong to kill.*

As he aimed the rifle, where was the image in his head of a disappointed mother or father, or of a teacher or coach or youth pastor or friend, or God?

When his finger squeezed the trigger, where was the thought of consequences—of his life and those of his victims being forever changed as those bullets found their target?

After the first student was hit, where was the sense of guilt that may have stopped his spree? And later, when taken into custody and he pulled a hidden knife on a deputy, where was his sense of shame and remorse?

The reality is this: If a kid wants to kill badly enough, no program or officer or counselor or security fence will stop him. The question, then, is, Why does a kid want to kill? The answer, I believe, lies deep in the human heart—deeper, at times, than outsiders will ever be able to discern.

I've read hundreds of thousands of words on the Springfield shooting, and little suggests that this was a case of a neglected son; as teachers and friends, the parents drew high marks from those who knew them. They lived in a nice, woodsy neighborhood. Their other child, an older daughter, seems the polar opposite of her brother, the suspect, courageously going on "20/20" with Barbara Walters and appearing as perplexed as anyone else about why he may have gone berserk.

At the same time, as parents we can't ignore the connection between ourselves and our children; we have, for better or worse, a huge role in who they ultimately become. Perhaps the Springfield case is an exception, but study after study done on young prisoners overwhelmingly shows weak family structure—not race, poverty, or lack of education—as their most common trait.

In the end, on that May morning, nobody pulled that trigger but the young man himself; he is responsible for those deaths. Likewise, when my sons make bad choices, they're responsible for those choices. Regardless, as a parent, I must constantly be assessing not only what I'm teaching my sons but, more importantly, what I'm modeling. As a parent, I'm called to help instill the kind of character in my sons that will help them choose right from wrong.

Like the proverbial archer, I cannot control the arrow once it's left the bow. But I'm called to communicate character to my sons, even if they choose not to listen. I'm called to show them what character looks like, even if they choose not to emulate me. And I'm called to continue loving them, even if they wander far from where they belong.

To some degree, I believe we are all prodigals who sometimes wander from where we belong. I believe the suspect in the Thurston incident wandered so far from home (i.e., his roots as part of a family, school, community, and God) that he felt no connection to anyone, including himself. And I believe it's our connections to one another—and to our Creator—that become our voice of conscience. That, were we to feel our finger on that trigger, would bring to mind consequences of pulling that trigger.

Therein lies the power of legacies. Legacies ground us to our ethical homes. Legacies are more than warm-and-fuzzy nostalgia, more than handed-down quilts and fly rods. They define us. They guide us. Most importantly, they show us, without robbing us of our individual bents, *how we are to act*. And too many young people are trying to make their way in the world without having been shown that.

A few months ago, I got a note from a young reporter whom I had taught in a journalism class at the University of Oregon. He had just avoided what would have been a serious mistake. He would have written a story about a man *nearly* drowning but, because he made a final call to the hospital right before deadline, learned that the man had actually died. Tragic though the outcome was, the reporter updated the story to reflect the truth; other papers did not.

He made that call, his note said, because he remembered a hypothetical car-wreck exercise in which I had emphasized the importance of making such last-minute calls—and later penalized him two full grades when he had not.

I thanked the young man for his note, but passed the credit on to an old journalism professor of mine who had taught me that same lesson by offering a similar hypothetical exercise—and similar punishment, which I wasn't particularly thrilled about at the time. And, of course, at some point someone had to have taught my professor that lesson, too.

In a sense, that's how legacies work: We put the missing pieces in someone else's puzzle, one generation to the next—at times, by caring enough to risk some short-term unpopularity for long-term results.

An 80-year-old woman eloquently captured the power of legacies in a story for *The Register-Guard*'s reader-produced "Write On" column.

"Before I was six, my father left a nickel on a windowsill in his bedroom to see if I had learned other people's property was to be respected," wrote Jessie Smith. "I looked at the nickel and thought about a strawberry ice cream cone. Then I thought about how nice his face would look if I left his nickel there where he put it; and I moved on to have tea with my dolls."

I presume that, nearly a century later, she still makes choices based on such thinking: that selfish desires should be outweighed by our chance to please someone else. Her father had cared enough about her to teach her a lesson. And that lesson would become like a reference book in Jessie Smith's mental library—something perhaps not often used, but there when she needed it.

I do not know why that reference guide wasn't there for the suspect in the Thurston case who so desperately needed it; in fact, short of finding some sort of mental or chemical imbalance in the young man, I doubt we'll ever know.

I do not know what values his parents tried to pass on to their son, and what he refused to accept. I only know that as I walked along that chain-link fence in front of the high school last May, past sobbing students and flowers and a note from a little girl that said, "sory for your tragity," I was not only sad but dismayed. Dismayed that a young man who seemingly had all the material and educational advantages could make such a tragically poor choice.

I hope that the next young man whose anger drives him to consider such actions—the next young man who ponders whether to take that nickel from the windowsill—is able to picture the face of someone he loves. And I hope that image will influence him to leave alone what doesn't belong to him: in this case, the lives of others.

Nurturing the Numbers

> I am careful not to thin my pines out too much because young trees grow best in crowds where they support each other in storms. By removing too many, the remainder are endangered by windthrow.
>
> —*The Trees in My Forest*

The plane touched down in Colorado Springs and, frankly, I was wishing I wasn't on it. For starters, the runway-to-terminal taxi in Colorado Springs seems so long that you think you've accidentally landed somewhere in Kansas by mistake.

But it was more than that. In the spring of 1997, *Focus on the Family Magazine* asked me to come to Colorado to interview and observe the Van Wingerdens, a family with 22 biological and adopted children. Part of my reluctance was that a book deadline was bearing down on me like a Mack truck in my rearview mirror. But to be honest, what I feared even more was what I would find when I walked into the Van Wingerdens' home: I feared I would find an out-of-control household with a dead-tired mother and enough Cheez-Its on the floor to feed an international mouse convention. And somehow I feared having to compromise the truth in making them look like the happy family *Focus on the Family* imagined.

That's not what I found. What I found shattered my misconceptions. Opened my eyes. Humbled my heart.

At the time, 20 of the 22 children—ranging in age from 23 to 1—lived at home. The numbers alone can strike fear into the heart of anyone who's ever tried to fix breakfast for a slumber-party gang or reffed a kids' battle for the bathroom. But getting to know Arie and Lynn Van Wingerden and their family was like entering an open house that you're cynical about, then finding yourself more enthralled with each room you see. Finally, you find yourself saying, "I really *like* this place."

This is a family that pipes in classical music each morning to wake the kids and get them ready for class (they're home-schooled) and church.

A family in which the children decided recently to forgo giving Christmas presents to each other so the money could be donated to missionaries.

A family in which each of the children has "adopted" a grandparent at a nearby nursing home. (OK, so they did arrive at the place one time and realize they had accidentally left eight-year-old Greg at home; you can't fault the effort.)

In some people's eyes, Lynn Van Wingerden is the Colorado woman with 22 children who holds up the line at the library because she is checking out 200 books (I'm not kidding), the woman whose life must be dawn-to-dusk drudgery because her household goes through 10 to 12 loads of laundry per day.

But in the eyes of Tony Van Wingerden, she's the one who said yes when everyone else said no to adopting a 15-year-old mentally retarded boy from Brazil—him.

And in the eyes of four-year-old Jordan Van Wingerden, she's the one who opened her heart and home when others said no to a week-old "crack baby" abandoned by his mother—him.

And in my eyes, she and Arie are offering love legacies to a bunch of children who may otherwise have gone without, not to mention inspiration to parents who struggle with raising only one or two children.

Lynn and Arie have opened their hearts and home to eight other orphans from Brazil and Haiti, and 12 children of their own, giving them a family so large that once, when the brood visited a museum, the host refused to give them a family discount, convinced they were actually a small school just trying to save money.

Drudgery? "These are my blessings," says Lynn, who lives with her family just north of Colorado Springs on 600 acres.

For Lynn, 40 at the time I visited, and Arie, 43, the idea of expanding their already-large family developed gradually. Arie was one of 16 children himself, so when the two married as high school sweethearts, a semi-precedent had been set. After their fifth child, they were sitting in church when they heard of a need for someone to take in three children whose leukemia-stricken mother needed a bone-marrow transplant.

The Van Wingerdens said yes. That opened the door to becoming foster parents, a challenge they found partially fulfilling but ultimately frustrating because of its temporary nature. When the couple decided to adopt children, they did so with little preparation. "We'd heard there was a need to adopt older kids from Brazil," says Lynn. "They asked us: 'Do you want a boy? A girl? Would you take a boy or girl who has physical or mental problems?' We just said send us someone who needs a home. We just want to help kids."

The family grew and grew. In 1993, with 19 children already in the Van Wingerden home, Lynn got a phone call at her then-suburban Philadelphia home. A social-service agency had a baby whose mother had abandoned him.

Because nobody would take the child, office workers were taking turns taking the baby home. Would she? Could she?

Yes.

But as soon as Lynn got young Jordan home, she realized something was different about this child. He cried incessantly. He vomited. He shook. He slept little. And finally, he came down with pneumonia.

At the hospital, a nurse who used to live in inner-city Philadelphia took one look at Jordan. "This," she says, "is a crack baby." Her only advice? Ride it out. For three months, Lynn did exactly that, withstanding day after day of Jordan trying to shake the symptoms of his mother's cocaine addiction. Finally, the raging storm ended in welcome calm.

"He's a sweetheart now, just perfect," says Lynn.

Not long ago, an agency called, wondering if the family would take another crack baby. The Van Wingerdens said yes. But the birth mother said no, deciding the family couldn't give her child enough individual attention.

Which begs the question: Is it possible to give so many children the individual attention they need?

"We try at every opportunity to make ourselves available to the kids," says Lynn. "Some of the older ones work with Arie (the family runs a large wholesale greenhouse business). I'll take one or two with me to go to the library or the store. But like parents with even a few kids, we have to really work at it."

In the mammoth nursery operation he runs, Arie has designed a mechanized watering system that, on paper, sounds impossible but, in practice, works wonderfully; so wonderfully, in fact, that his system is sold around the country. I've seen it. Rather than someone taking a hose to the thousands of plants, the plants come to the water: they move along a motorized chain, like a chair lift, stop, and—*phhhht*—receive their daily dose from a fixed water faucet that's programmed to give each plant the amount of water it needs.

In a sense, that is how you make a family of 22 work: You design a nurturing system that may look different than most others, but nevertheless provides each child with the nourishment he or she needs.

Lynn home-schools the 13 school-age children with help from two part-time teachers and the older children. A special-education teacher helps three of the children who struggle. And art and piano teachers come once a week to the family's 12,000-square-foot house, which includes a 10,000-volume library.

The buddy system is used extensively. For example, every Saturday night older children know which children they're to get ready for church the next morning. Clothes are picked out in advance. The family travels in two vans: one 15-passenger vehicle and one minivan.

After church they've been known to stop and eat at a country buffet. "It's cheaper than even McDonald's because they offer a 'pay-by-the-year' setup for the kids," says Lynn. The usual bill is 115 dollars to 120 dollars. "Of course, that's assuming that my husband gets the bus driver's discount," she says, laughing.

She's found other ways to make special events more economical. "I found it costs our entire family about 80 dollars to go to the zoo one time, but if we buy a family membership, we can pay 50 dollars and go whenever we want." The family's weekly food bill runs between 500 dollars and 700 dollars.

If money can be challenging, so can time. But again, the Van Wingerdens find a way. Lynn and Arie occasionally go out for dinner alone—it's not like they don't have a few babysitters to choose from. The whole family sometimes vacations at the beach. (Don't even ask how they pull that one off.)

But the Van Wingerden family is about more than day-to-day logistics. It's about children growing up feeling loved by God, parents, and siblings (some of the children even make get-well cards for each other when they're sick). It's about the security of a home. It's about living for something beyond our own personal comfort.

It's about children who, even when you talk to them away from their parents, express a warmth and security that I never expected. As if they thought everybody had loving parents and enough siblings to form a couple of football teams.

In a quiet moment—yes, we found a few of them—I ask Lynn if she would do it over again. In a heartbeat, she says. In fact, she and Arie are considering further expansion.

"There's such a stigma against children in our culture," she says. "People will say kids just get in the way, they bottle up your time, they make you lose your figure, they make you run out of money. The Bible talks about children as blessings, about taking care of orphans and widows. That's what we're doing here. We've got a life that's much more than 'what's-in-it-for-me?'

"If you're blessed financially, you wouldn't go to the bank and say, 'Don't put any more money in my account.' So if children are blessings, why should we do that for children and say, 'Don't put any more children in my house'?"

In ten years, I hope to check back and see what's happened to Lynn and Arie's 22 blessings. In the meantime, when I think of that family, I don't picture the image I thought would represent them—that of a harried mother overwrought with needy children.

Instead, I picture a family bonded by a love that goes beyond blood. Adults and children who seem acutely aware that each of them is an integral part of the whole. A husband and wife whom God has blessed materially, and yet willingly forsake "the good life" for what they clearly see as a better life.

Instead, I picture four-year-old Jordan, the "crack baby" nobody wanted, jumping on a trampoline with the Rocky Mountains in front of him as wide as his huge eyes can see. And how the little boy who once couldn't stop crying in pain now is so full of life he can't stop laughing with joy.

Greener Pastures

> To keep roots from harm, each plant should be moved with as much soil around its roots as possible. In this way, the plant travels from place to place wrapped in its familiar environment, remaining within it until it is confident enough to grow out into what lies beyond.
>
> —*Bringing a Garden to Life*

When we moved from the mom-and-pop-ness of Bend, Oregon, to the brie-and-wine-ness of Bellevue, Washington, my wife and I felt a disconnectedness like we had never felt before. It was 1983. Our children were four and one. And we were lonely.

Professionally, it had been a step to greener pastures, but we missed lots of things about our old lives: the unpretentious small-town life, friends with whom we had begun our parenting careers, and traffic so light that on snowy days I would occasionally strap on my cross-country skis and glide through Drake Park to the newspaper where I worked. But mainly what we missed was family.

In Bend, we had been a couple of hours and a mountain pass away from most of our relatives. Now we were six hours and a couple of cultural time zones away. Day trips home were out of the question; weekend trips home were still impractical, particularly with traffic making Seattle seem like L.A. North.

What's more, we had difficulty feeling as if we fit in this new environment. Bellevue, for the uninitiated, is the land of milk and honey. It's in the backyard of such world headquarters as Microsoft, Nintendo, and Boeing. Your neighbor might be software billionaire Bill Gates, who plunked down a cool 50 million dollars for his lakeside fixer-upper. ("Uh, hi, Bill, we just moved into the rental down the street and wondered if we could borrow a cup of sugar.") Reports of Bellevue fire hydrants storing Perrier, not water, may have been exaggerated, but I kid you not: I once went to a garage sale that accepted Visa and Mastercard.

I'm sure we were the only people in the city who rented a house, had one car, and had a refrigerator in our entryway. (It wouldn't fit into the kitchen, and we had no other place to put it; "Welcome, can I get you something to drink—like right this very instant?")

If one can feel exiled amid affluence, that's how we felt. Everything seemed big and fast and gaudy. We saw more Mercedes cars in our church parking lot one Sunday morning than we had seen in seven years in Bend. We could go months without seeing people we knew—in our own church. After attending a young-marrieds Sunday school class for six months, we were introduced as "new people" because nobody recognized us. It was, we decided, time to find a smaller church.

Amid this change in environment, Sally unwrapped a gift given to her from Gram Klein, another one of Sally's grandparents who had once lived on a dairy farm. It was a couple of porcelain cows. Kind of goofy-looking porcelain cows, I thought.

But to Sally they were more than a couple of cows; she welcomed them as a soldier in some far-off land might welcome a tin of homemade chocolate chip cookies. They were links to her roots of having been raised on a farm. They were reminders of our identity. And they were, at least on some subconscious level, like a rainbow from God: a sign of hope for the future, a promise. If we could survive this place's flood of materialism, He would never put us through this again. In the meantime, He seemed to be saying, "Patience; there's life beyond Perrier."

As our time in Bellevue stretched on, Sally started adorning our rental with more cows. Stuffed. Glass. Wood. Some that mooed. Some whose legs kicked up when you pulled a string. But most did what cows mainly do: nothing.

Friends and family picked up on her heifer habit and started giving cows as gifts. Sally started subscribing to a "cowtalog," in which she could buy cow prints and mugs and stationery and hats. She started a small cow-making business. One year, our Christmas card-photo was taken of the four of us in a field of grazing cows.

When we had first moved into our rental, what you noticed was the pea-green carpet and the black mirror tiles on the dining-room wall; it was as if we lived in a cheap Chinese restaurant. But now it looked more like a dairy farm—in a good sort of way.

Weeks became months. Months became years. Finally, a job offer came to me from an Oregon paper that I had wanted to work at ever since I worked at it part-time in college. Nearly seven years after moving into this rental, we were, in essence, going home.

Looking back, it strikes me that we were essentially the same family when we left as when we came. Oh sure, we had a second car—a '76 Rabbit with grass growing in the back floorboards. And a boat—an eight-foot dinghy that we lashed to the back of the U-Haul. But I don't think we were any more materialistic than when we arrived.

Part of that was because, in those years, we each had the opportunity to spend time in Haiti, the most impoverished country in the Western Hemisphere. Those experiences gave us perspective. Except for the hillside houses of the political and military leaders that looked down on the cinder-block houses of Port-au-Prince, our Bellevue rental would be considered among the most elite abodes on the island.

But a large part, I think, was that Sally's sense of heritage—yes, a heritage represented by heifers—helped keep us focused on who we were, where we had come from, and to whom we belonged. Her roots were so important to her that she refused to forget them. When you're grounded like that, you're less likely to be swayed by the changing norms of time and place. And that's what dilutes so many legacies—not that they haven't been lovingly bequeathed or lovingly accepted, but that they can't survive the trauma of transplanting.

Finally, a part of our sustenance was our faith, which remained our rock amid the changes. Proclaims Psalm 103:11,12: "For as high as the heavens are above the earth, so great is his love for those who fear him; as far as the east is from the west, so far has he removed our transgressions from us." In other words, God's love and forgiveness of us transcend both time and place; wherever we go, it follows, hidden in our hearts.

Legacies, Sally and I learned, can transcend not only changing times and changing technology, but changing places. No better example of that exists than that of Jewish people. They were the world's homeless, scattered for thousands of years. They've endured hatred, bigotry, even attempts at racial genocide. But Jews have maintained a glue-like connection with their faith and with each other because *where* they were was never as important as *who* they were.

In one sense, Sally and her cows became the silent keepers of our family's flame. The symbol of a sort of no-frills life-style that her parents and grandparents had instilled in her when she was young. And a reminder that, when moving, some of the most important stuff to bring along isn't found inside your boxes, but inside your heart.

My Evening with Andre

In 1967, botanists thawed the seeds of an arctic tundra lupine frozen for 10,000 years in a lemming burrow; they germinated within 48 hours.

—*North American Trees*

I was filled with enthusiasm and great expectations. Our car was filled with gas and fresh coolant, necessities for a hot-afternoon drive that would lead to a book- signing I was doing.

The event would take place at seven o'clock that evening at a major-chain bookstore in Portland, two hours from our home in Eugene. As we headed north, I envisioned a throng of book-buyers lined up for autographs. I envisioned the store's host thanking me for having the foresight to bring extra books. I envisioned a little sign on my Ford Explorer's dashboard saying: *Check Engine*.

Hold it! This last image wasn't something I envisioned. The little sign was actually saying that: *Check Engine*. I looked at the engine temperature gauge. It was leaning farther right than Rush Limbaugh.

"Do you smell something—something hot?" asked Sally.

"We're overheating," I said and, with the composure of a madman who has hijacked a busload of Cub Scouts and is being pursued by an entire state police force, steered toward the nearest exit.

"But I just had the fluids topped off yesterday," said Sally.

Some things just don't make sense. Why me, Lord? Why now? Why here? Why do I drive a vehicle for 61,000 miles without having it overheat, and then have it start vomiting green stuff when I'm on the brink of one of life's more significant moments? Why doesn't the car overheat when I'm driving a mile from home or, say, when I'm driving by my mechanic's garage on my lunch hour?

We were 25 miles from the bookstore during Friday afternoon rush-hour traffic and limped into a car-wash parking lot, our coolant puddling on the asphalt.

What to do? Traffic around us was bumper-to-bumper. We saw no service stations. And we had 90 minutes to get to the bookstore on the other side of Portland. I found a phone booth. The first towing service I reached helped people with overheated vehicles but had nobody in the area. The second service had a truck in the area but didn't service cars, only towed them. The third delivered pizza (I had gotten a wrong number).

I ran back across the street, considering the possibilities of a cab. What could it cost? Fifty bucks? Seventy-five? Was it worth it?

I assessed the situation and then did what I should have done first: said a prayer. I would like to tell you it was one of those St. Francis of Assisi prayers or Dietrich Bonhoeffer prayers, or even one of those nice, fuzzy "grant-me-the-courage" prayers that you see on refrigerator magnets. But it was actually more like: "God, I'm clueless. If I'm meant to get to this book-signing, please get me there on time. Show me the way. Thanks."

The sky did not open up to release shafts of heavenly light accompanied by a choir of angels singing "Follow Us," with a golden chariot whose electronic placard read "Barnes & Noble." Instead, a portly guy from the car wash moseyed out and asked if I could use some water for the radiator.

I thought the problem was more serious, perhaps a faulty thermostat, given that we had just had the fluids topped off the previous day. But I also figured I might need to take a risk.

"Sure," I said.

We started the car and filled the radiator. The needle registered semihot instead of up-the-creek hot. We headed out, by now having only an hour to get through this gridlock. To make matters worse, I missed a bridge turnoff to cross the Willamette River, meaning we had to go through downtown, whose traffic on this hot afternoon was like a billion ants on a waffle iron. But somehow we got over the river and through the traffic to where we needed to be.

I arrived at the bookstore hot and sweaty, but I arrived. Sally headed to other stores to do some shopping. I rushed in and introduced myself to the host of the event. He was a young man named Andre. He promptly announced over the store's public-address system that the author of *A Father for All Seasons*, Bob Woods, would start signing books now.

Bob *Woods*? Oh well. I was here. That was the important thing. Bring on the throngs.

"Sometimes, things start a little slow," said Andre, noticing, as I did, that nobody was awaiting us in the book-signing area.

The two of us chatted as I awaited the hungry autograph hounds. Five minutes passed, then ten, fifteen. It appeared the hounds weren't all that hungry on this hot summer evening. Or maybe they were just hungry hounds stuck in traffic; yeah, that was probably it.

Groping for common ground, I started making small talk with Andre. My book was about fathers, so that seemed like a good start. He said something about not even knowing who his father was until he was a teenager, but I wasn't listening too intently as I had my ear figuratively to the ground, awaiting sounds of the stampede.

I soon realized a stampede might be asking a bit much. I lowered my expectations from a stampede of book-seekers to a pack, then to a handful. Finally, I started hoping that perhaps one person would walk up and ask for a signed book, even if by accident, even if he or she thought I was someone else, like the author of *A Gourmet's Guide to Goat Cheese*.

"So anyway, when my daughter was born, it's like, whoa, how am I supposed to be a dad? I never had a dad show me how to be one. Does your book talk about that?"

What? Andre's intensity caught me off guard. Where were the book-buyers anyway?

"Now, me and my wife," he went on, "well, we've been kind of struggling lately. Actually, I'm not sure if we're going to make it."

Then I saw it: His eyes were growing slightly misty. Seeing him and hearing him—really, for the first time—my eyes grew clear. My vision had been clouded by my own ego. I realized that as I had been making small talk, Andre had been making big talk. I had been looking for numbers, strokes; he had been looking for answers, hope.

"Did you say you went to Grant High?" I asked him.

"Yeah."

"That's where my father graduated from, way back in '42. Long before your time."

"Really?"

"Yeah, I wrote this book soon after he died last year. He grew up at 29th and Fremont. And his father, my grandfather, used to play baseball for the old Williams Avenue School back around the turn of the century."

"Sure, I know where Williams Avenue is."

"By that hospital."

"Yeah, Providence Hospital."

"Right."

For the next 45 minutes, I had perhaps the most fascinating conversation with a stranger that I've ever had. We were two very different people. I was 44; he was 29. I was white; he was black. I had been raised in an intact family in a middle-class university town; he had been raised by a God-fearing mother on Portland's gang-riddled east side.

But we went from nowhere to somewhere in a matter of minutes. We talked about marriage, fatherhood, and faith; about what influences people to be who they are, about what's important in life.

As our talk deepened, I started hoping that nobody would walk up and spoil our time together by asking for a signed book. We talked about Andre growing up with a man he thought was his father, only to discover as a teenager that his real father was someone else. We talked about trust. And about my belief that God was the foundation we needed for our lives, and how easily lives washed away when built on such non-God stuff as pride, power, politics, materialism, and self.

"You have a chance," I said, "to do what your father could not, or would not, do for you: leave your daughter with a loving legacy. You have a chance to start a new chapter in your family's life, to take that good stuff your mom passed down to you and to pass it on to your daughter."

I paused. He digested. "But it begins with loving her mother, your wife. Dropping your pride. Making her feel she's the most important person in the world. It's hard. I know, because I regularly fail at it."

He sat there for a moment. I didn't know if I had offended him, enlightened him, or both. "I never thought of that," he said. "Nobody's ever talked to me about this kind of stuff before."

We talked more. Then it was 8 o'clock, time for the "signing" to end.

"Thanks," he said.

"Thank you," I said.

I gave him a book. We shook hands, exchanged addresses, and went our separate ways, probably never to see one another again. I don't know how much the conversation meant to him. I don't know if anything I said changed his life in the least, if it inspired him in some small way to rededicate himself to the roles of husband and father. But maybe—just maybe—it was a start.

Some honorable legacies lie dormant for generations, waiting—just waiting—to germinate in a new generation. Maybe on his legacy tree, Andre would be the first bud to blossom in a long, long time.

Not one person showed up to get an autographed copy of my book that evening. I had been skunked, blanked, the victim of a no-hit shutout. But rather than feeling humiliated, I felt strangely honored to have spent time with this guy. Later, Sally would tell me that midway through the evening she was going to join the two of us but sensed, from a distance, that something important was happening. She browsed instead.

Thinking back, I remember how I had stood in front of that car wash, praying my feeble prayer to get me to this bookstore if it was meant to be. Obviously, it was.

Broken Hearts

> Windstorms break limbs and open the way to decay. Drought reduces resistance. Too much water cuts down oxygen for roots. Impoverished soil, lacking nutrients, weakens resistance. But what is the greatest single cause of…losses by disease in forest stands? Heart rot.
>
> —*1001 Questions Answered About Trees*

It happened during one of those Rockwellian moments: a grandmother making cookies with her seven-year-old granddaughter. The kind of moment a grandmother wraps around her like a handmade shawl, to keep her warm months later, when the smell of Snickerdoodles no longer fills the kitchen, and the child has returned to another time zone.

The little girl, the grandmother noticed, was engrossed in the flour. She had a knife and, with the intensity of a sculptor—a sculptor whose little tongue suggested she was deep in concentration—carefully shaped the fine powder into a pattern of neat, narrow lines.

How cute, the woman remembers thinking. Then the little girl looked up at her. "Look, Grandma," she said, "this is how Mom and Gary cut their cocaine."

I met this grandmother and her husband while researching a story about grandparents forced to raise their grandchildren because their adult children weren't responsible enough. In such cases, the parents were too strung out on drugs or too enslaved by alcohol, perhaps both. Maybe they were in jail. Or maybe they simply up and left, abandoning their child or children in search of the officially sanctioned god of the sixties generation: self-fulfillment.

Honorable legacies die for a number of reasons, among them selfishness and neglect. Baby boomers aren't the first generation to succumb to self-absorption and, judging from their successors, may not be the last. But my generation has taken it to new heights—or depths.

What kind of legacies do me-first people leave? A generation of children struggling to tell right from wrong. A generation of children robbed of innocence. A generation of children trying desperately to survive in impoverished soil.

Our culture idolizes pleasure, comfort, and independence—ingredients that undermine parenting with long-range perspective. "We have a generation of parents out there that's producing babies but never learned to be responsible to the degree they need to be," a childhood educator told me. "It's the Me Generation. Drugs fit that generation's instant-gratification bent; children do not."

The result? By 1995, the number of children being raised by their grandparents would fill 30 stadiums the size of the Rose Bowl; according to the U.S. Census Bureau, 3.3 million children were in such living situations, a 41 percent increase in *just the last 15 years*.

I applaud the parental fill-ins; like weary marathoners whose race is over, they suddenly find themselves called back to the starting line. But I anguish over the fact that, in a culture so materially blessed, it has come to this: children growing up in a world where "normal" means lines of cocaine and, ultimately, 65-year-old guardians.

Such selfishness shows its face in a myriad of other ways, and far beyond the blue-collar world. Consider the 1998

Sports Illustrated article on children fathered out of wedlock by players in the National Basketball Association—players who enjoy a fame and fortune that few will ever experience. More children have been fathered out of wedlock by current NBA players, estimated one agent, than the number of NBA players in the entire league. One player, who had recently signed an 84 million dollar deal that was the richest contract in league history, was supporting five children by four women. Another had had three children by three women before he had turned 21.

What kind of legacies do these "heroes" leave their children? Children wearing their father's jersey, but never knowing the man behind the number. Children whose most intimate contact with the man will come from the confinement of a TV screen. Children with little oxygen to nurture their roots.

One in four children is born out of wedlock. Half will grow up in a home broken by divorce. Discussing the latter, I realize, is like dropping bombs on an enemy; no matter how closely you pinpoint your target, innocent people still get wounded. My intention isn't to slap some sort of scarlet letter on those whose families aren't the stuff of minivan commercials or to suggest that victims of divorce are doomed to lives of unfulfillment. In particular, mothers forced to raise their children alone need support, not condemnation. But to ignore the painful legacy of marital breakups is to suggest that it's somehow more important to protect the feelings of adults who waged the war than the innocent children who get caught in the cross fire.

To understand the legacy of divorce, you can dig up studies, quote statistics, and peruse surveys that have piled up like cancer research. You can read Barbara Dafoe Whitehead's *The Culture of Divorce*, based on her award-winning

1993 article in *Atlantic Monthly*, in which she tweaked the culturally elite with her kids-need-a-mom-and-dad-at-home argument.

Or you can listen to those who inherit its legacy: the children themselves. Like the high school girl who's part of a group of teenage journalists I supervise at the newspaper where I work. For a story about growing up in homes hit by divorce, she wrote:

> The worst effect this whole deal has had on me is my fear of commitment. Although I rarely confess to it, I am deathly afraid of committing myself to a relationship. Partly because I'm afraid of making a mistake. Mostly because I'm afraid of giving my heart and my life to another person, and having it returned in an unopened box, broken.

Wrote another girl:

> I was an accidental pregnancy. When I volunteered for this assignment, I thought it would be effortless to write. I thought that my parents' divorce didn't have much impact on my life. But then I laid awake at night thinking about the divorce and how it's affected me. I remembered things vividly that I had long forgotten. I became annoyed, frustrated, and tried to go to sleep. But I couldn't. I realized that I had been in denial all my life. I was finally being truthful with myself.
>
> I don't know what it's like to have a relationship with a father. Because of the impact my real dad has had on me, I am cautious and untrusting toward most men beyond my peers. Because I never have experienced a loving relationship with my dad, I don't really miss it. But I do wonder what it's like.

She wrote that piece a year ago. In recent months, I noticed a drop in the number of stories she had written, a listlessness in columns that once sang, a hesitancy to speak out in meetings. After one such gathering, I asked her if something in my leadership or something about the team was dragging her down.

She started to cry. And then softly revealed that her mother was going through yet another divorce. "I want to do so much better in my writing," she said, "but I'm so stressed I don't have any emotional energy left to write."

What kind of legacies does divorce leave to many children? Children whose creative voices grow quiet. Children afraid of hearts and lives coming back in unopened boxes. Children for whom windstorms have left broken limbs and opened the way to decay.

If wind and fire can devastate a forest, insects and diseases are far more common threats. And so it is with families, which are more often weakened by the insidious spread of neglect than anything else.

Neglect often is rooted in our being too busy. In this country, being busy is next to godliness. It is the mark of success, the barometer of significance, the testament of commitment to the graven image of the American Dream. And it's producing a fascinating backlash in children.

In November 1998, *New York Times Magazine* reported that kids now consider stay-at-home moms the "ultimate trophy."

> "That which enhances prestige in the grown-up world—degrees, money, stylish clothes, power—fails to register on (children's) radar. Indeed, a recent survey of 6- to 17-year-olds by the Whirlpool Foundation revealed that out of 15 possible characteristics of the 'ideal' mother, having an important job was ranked 14th." Said one of the children: "The coolest mom I know who's not mine is Connor's. She plays soccer with him all the time. I don't think she has a job. She cooks."

I could be more smug about such discoveries were I not a recovering workaholic myself. I've struggled with being overcommitted since the mid-eighties, when I purchased my first computer and decided I would not only work for a newspaper, but would write free-lance articles and books as well, and speak to various groups when given the opportunity. A recent incident jolted home the painful truth that I still sometimes bow to the idol of accomplishments.

My wife was on her way to the Dominican Republic on a short-term medical mission, and I had one thing on my mind: to immerse myself for two weeks in launching the book you're reading now. After dropping her off with friends who would take her to the airport, I headed home, remembering to stop on the way and pick up my teenage son, Jason, after baseball practice.

He wasn't at the baseball field. I drove home, assuming he had gotten a ride with someone else. He wasn't there. I started making some phone calls. He wasn't with any of his friends that I could reach. I headed back to the school and checked out the basketball game that I suspected he might have stopped to watch. He wasn't there.

I talked to people at the game; nobody had seen him. I started to panic. I raced home again. Made more phone calls. By now, more than an hour had passed since I first stopped by the school. Finally, our phone rang: It was him. He had walked to a friend's house and wanted me to know where he was.

"Stay put," I said. "I'm coming to get you."

"But, Dad, I—"

"Stay put!"

I slammed down the phone. I wasn't relieved. I wasn't thankful. I was mad. I had great plans to jump-start this project on this particular evening, and I was spending most of it on a phone and in a car. My anger surged from head to foot and I was beyond the 25 MPH speed limit as I twisted through an S-curve that fronted a church. Suddenly, in the darkness, a handful of people were in my headlights, crossing the street.

I slammed on my brakes. The people scrambled toward the sidewalk. As I drove by, narrowly missing two of them, I saw in my rearview mirror a man angrily shaking his fist at me. I turned the corner, drove to the side of the street, buried my face in my hands, and wept.

My meltdown was more than spontaneous fear at having nearly run down a group of people. My meltdown was born of shame. The shame you feel when realizing that you've placed your own selfish desires far ahead of others, that you've become some sort of madman driven by a to-do list.

In the six months since his brother had left for college and he had become the lone child at home, Jason and I had been slightly out of synch with one another; in a sense, the father-son trio had become the father-son duo, and we were still trying to find a new rhythm. But as I had searched for him earlier, that didn't matter in the least; I desperately had wanted to find him safe.

So why, when I finally heard my son was OK, did I not rejoice and thank God? Like the father of the prodigal son, why did I not celebrate, realizing that my son was lost, but now he's found?

Instead, I seethed because I had lost two hours' time on a book that my son won't remember nearly as vividly as he will the time I took to be with him, or the time my anger exploded on the other end of a phone line.

I once interviewed a well-heeled man who desperately wanted to believe he was connected to his teenage son, but couldn't even tell me what high school the young man attended.

I once knew a woman who was climbing the corporate ladder in one of the country's hottest high-tech regions, then one day realized she was a total stranger to her teenage daughter.

I once saw a newspaper photograph that showed a young boy fishing at a Montana lake while his father, some 30 feet away, compiled a business report on a laptop computer. I cut it out and pinned it to my wall at work as a reminder to never become that father, because though his son might not say it, he clearly knew what his dad's priority was on this "father-son" outing.

But on the night of my meltdown, I was no different from any of these people. When you race through life, you can hurt innocent people. Being too busy can ruin the very thing God made us for: relationships.

What kind of legacies do overcommitted people leave their children? We leave children who will remember being less important to their parents than a laptop, a client, a manuscript. We leave children who will find other people—in extreme cases, in prisons and gangs—to replace what parents did not give. We leave children whose resistance has been reduced by drought.

Such anecdotes raise lots of questions about the legacies we leave when we put self above others. But the most important question is, What do we do with the realization that we're not all we should be?

Our choices are two: We can allow shame to petrify into guilt. Like a diseased tree, our growth can be stymied by heart rot, a sort of hardening of our emotional arteries; in essence, we can give up. Or just as the first autumn cold snap triggers a collage of colors, we can allow our brokenness to trigger vibrant change in who we are and how we parent.

Soon after my meltdown with Jason, our family was at the coast.

"Jason," I said, "How 'bout a walk?"

"Huh?"

"You and me. Let's walk."

In the 16 years I had been the boy's father, I had read to him, coached him, and taken him to more games than the beach has shells. But I don't believe I had ever asked him to simply take a walk—just him and me. He quickly did a mental scan disk, perhaps searching for hidden agendas in this apparent program upgrade. Finding none, he put on his shoes. And as the waves crashed on the rocks, we walked. We talked.

Long pauses sometimes separated our words. The conversation was stilted at times, nothing like in the movies. But we learned some things about one another, about Jason sometimes feeling his brother got more attention than he did, about me sometimes feeling Jason was pulling away too fast from Sally and me.

It was not cinematic stuff. No John Williams music welled up in the background and no movie credits started rolling upward in the sky above the ocean. But every legacy must start somewhere or start anew somewhere. And for me and my youngest son, this was that somewhere.

Weathering Time

Endurance

Some individual bristlecone pines have survived as many as 5,000 winters, making them Earth's oldest living species.

—*Trees of North America*

Over the years, I've watched them come into the newspapers where I've worked: husbands and wives in their sixties, seventies, eighties, and nineties, having come to fill out fiftieth-wedding anniversary forms and perhaps get their pictures taken for the Sunday paper. The women look lovely, as if this were a day they've had circled on their calendar for months. The men look less inspired, as if this were a day that's caused them minor indigestion for months. Some follow their wives in and out of the building as if they were boat trailers being pulled by cars.

I've noticed something else, however. If you congratulate such a couple on their achievement, the man will at first looked surprised, but as you shake his hand, he will suddenly stand up just a bit taller and maybe break into a little smile, as if first realizing that he and his wife have accomplished something noteworthy.

Endurance—the ability to withstand hardship, adversity or stress—is one of the most remarkable legacies someone can bequeath to those who follow. It says: *I did it; so can you.* It says: *Persevere.* It says: *Fight the good fight.*

But endurance, as something honorable, fares poorly in a here-and-now world. As a culture, we've become like the backseat children who shrug at the sight of a redwood forest and shout at the sight of the golden arches—slow to appreciate that which has been seasoned by time and quick to embrace that which seemingly popped up overnight.

The golden weds who walk into the newspaper find themselves like strangers in a strange land, living in a culture that celebrates youth, power, freedom, and glitz—not wisdom, patience, responsibility, and grit.

We honor the hollow, not the hallowed. In my hometown, mini-malls, quicky-lubes, and tanning salons pop up like weeds—while the college's museum closes for lack of funding. We lust for immediate comfort and convenience, and think little of long-term consequences.

A few years ago, an unknown author became an overnight success with the publishing of *The Bridges of Madison County*. For all that it dripped of romance and rightness, at its core the story was simple: unfulfilled farm wife has affair with self-absorbed free-lance photographer.

Millions read the book. Millions more saw the movie. And judging from the reactions I heard and read, most found the story fulfilling. Never mind dishonesty and betrayal. Never mind the consequences to a husband and children. Never mind the disregard for anything but "the moment." To read the reviews or listen to those who read the book or saw the movie, the couple was somehow heroic because, in reflecting one of Hollywood's threadbare themes, they "followed their hearts."

I'm a blessed man. I never had parents or in-laws or grandparents who lived in a paperback novel or in a Hollywood movie. Instead, I had parents and in-laws and grandparents who lived in the real world. They were real people who faced decades of real challenges and overcame those challenges with real character.

I had a grandfather—my father's father—whose alcoholic dad beat and abused his mother, but overcame that painful legacy to become a good and faithful husband and father.

I have in-laws who raised four happy, well-adjusted children, including my wife. My father-in-law started out as a small-time farmer, earned a Ph.D. in agronomy and, though now retired, still flies around the world as a consultant to help less-advanced countries improve their agricultural methods.

I have a mother who stuck with my father through a war, job losses, heart bypass surgeries, and an automobile accident that left her hospitalized off and on for nearly eight months. When you have tubes in your chest and a stomach so shredded that no food will pass through it, you don't feel a whole lot like slow-dancing in a Hollywood farmhouse. But you do learn a thing or two about true love and loyalty, particularly about those marriage vows that speak of "sickness and in health."

I'm a blessed man. Between Sally and me, our parents and four sets of grandparents have been or were married for an average of 52 years. Not a single leaf on our immediate branches has fallen to divorce since my great-grandmother and great-grandfather split around the turn of the century.

In a world adrift, they have been the rocks. In a world of style, they have been substance. In a world of neglect, they have been sustainers.

In 1938, Sally's grandparents and others on that family-tree level began a family reunion that has now lasted 60 years. Only once has an annual gathering been skipped; that, because of a death.

Such reunions give us identity. In Ephesians, Paul reminds us of our heritage: You belong to God, he says; therefore, live in a manner worthy of that. In the same way, reunions seem to say, "You belong to this family; therefore, live in a manner worthy of that." They anchor us to some ideal, some standard, some expectation that we should each carry on. And they remind us to appreciate those who have come before us, for just as there is value in change, so is there value in permanence.

A cousin of Sally's, Ron Hood, compares his baby-boom generation to the grandparents the two of them had in common:

> I only really knew Gram and Pop for the last 30 years of their lives, but during that time nothing much seemed to change. Same house, same church, same jobs....By some standards, they were in a rut, but as I look at my 20-year adult life, I've lived in eight or ten different communities, attended as many different churches, held four or five different jobs, and made and left more friends than I can count. I try and counter that nomadic life by emphasizing our anchor in Christ, our immediate and greater family, and commitment to our local church. Still, we've given up something in pursuit of "career growth" and I'm not always convinced it was a fair exchange.

Gram and Pop's generation spun off the World War II generation—a generation that anchorman Tom Brokaw calls "The Greatest Generation." In his book titled the same, he says we have much to learn from the generation that came of age in the Great Depression, people who are now in their seventies and eighties. "Their lessons," he writes, "may help all of us move to higher ground."

It's time we appreciated the generations that have come before us. They haven't been perfect, but they've fought to defend our country's freedom, stood for right and wrong, and accepted the sometimes-bitter pills of life with dignity.

The couples who come into the office to turn in their anniversary information haven't come from Madison County. They've come from Real America. Like my parents or in-laws, or maybe yours, they're people who nurtured their family with grit and grace; who endured; who, in some cases, loved each other enough to *not* always follow their hearts—which, at times, probably said, *Flee. Leave. Seek revenge.* For hearts are not always as pure as Hollywood would have us believe. And romance is not always as resilient when the wind is real, and not coming from offstage blowers.

The anniversary couples deserve more than four-inch stories and one-column photos in Sunday's paper. They deserve respect from the generations that follow. For their legacy is one of endurance. And there is honor in that.

Remembering

> A tree is shaped by its experiences...a record of what has happened to it becomes inscribed in its body. Wrinkles in the bark reflect age. Branch thickness indicates the loads it has carried and the direction from which it has experienced light. Scars remain where overloaded branches broke off.
>
> —*The Trees in My Forest*

When I was in my late twenties, I went to the dentist to have a routine cavity filled. It was more painful than I expected and I was more tense than usual, but finally the procedure ended.

"All done," said the dentist. "You can close your mouth now."

There was only one problem: My mouth would not close.

"I ah oh ie ow," I said, trying to tell him "I can't close my mouth."

"What?"

"I ah oh ie ow," I repeated.

He tried gently with his hands to coax the jaw shut. No dice. He huddled with his assistant, pulled out a pen, and scrawled the address of an oral surgeon's office on a piece of paper.

So there I was, driving across Bend, Oregon, with my mouth stuck open. When I pulled up to stoplights, people in the lane next to me would look at me and furrow their brows, then start laughing. I think they thought I was singing the last note of some opera—a really long last note. I would try to smile and act inconspicuous, which is not easy when you're in this condition.

I thought about how I could drown in my own saliva, then decided it was a bad idea, given how nobody wants the epitaph on his grave marker to say: "He drowned in his own spit. What a loser."

I thought about how strange it was that the doctor didn't have someone else drive me, and how if something happened to me—say, I broadsided a car in some intersection—I could probably sue the dentist and win, if I were the suing type and if I were still the alive type.

But mainly I thought about getting to this oral surgeon so I could get my mouth closed. It was hard to swallow, and I started to panic. I pulled in front of the medical building, raced inside, and said—well, what can you really say when your mouth is stuck open?

I motioned to the receptionist for a pencil and quickly scrawled: "I was sent by Dr. Black."

She frowned a very strange frown.

"Do you know this is a gynecology office?" she said.

My eyes grew wide. I looked around. Women, many of them pregnant, were staring at me from the waiting room. I stared back, openmouthed.

I took the paper and wrote the name of the oral surgeon I was to see.

"Oh," she said. "Next door."

I raced next door. The oral surgeon gave me Valium, waited for my body to relax, put me up against the wall, and pushed sideways on my jaw. My mouth closed. "There we go," he said. "You just had a dislocated jaw."

Oh, is that all?

Because of the Valium, I was unable to drive, so I called my wife. She was not home. So I called a friend. He was not home, but his wife said she could come pick me up. An hour later, we pulled up in front of my house. I staggered out of the woman's car, the Valium still making me drowsy, my tie loosened, my speech slightly slurred. My wife hurried onto the front porch. She looked at me. She looked at the woman. She looked puzzled.

"What—"

"Don't ask," I said.

❧ ❧ ❧

Family trees don't record stories like these. But legacy trees do. Legacy trees record all the wonderful (and not-so-wonderful) stuff that you said and did. And when you're gone, it becomes the stuff by which you're remembered. Because legacies are passed on mainly by stories.

I don't want anyone to ever forget that story because it seems to be quintessential *me*. It is the kind of thing that happens to me and not to someone else. And it needs to be preserved, like a box of tacky clothes, for special occasions.

I want to leave a legacy to my sons and their children of who I was. And I want to help my sons leave their own legacies of who they were.

On June 23, 1979, when *The Bulletin* newspaper in Bend hit our front porch, its entire front page was devoted to one event. "Ryan P. Welch arrives on time!" shouted the lead headline. Every story focused on Sally giving birth to our first child. Every photo related to the new arrival.

Such is the benefit of working at a small-town newspaper, where your colleagues not only occasionally produce souvenir front pages, but actually have the page run on the press, incorporated into your evening paper, and delivered to your door.

It is among the many items that have already been passed on to our oldest son, who is now 19 and needs to remember such events. In a sense, we are all a collection of stories from our pasts that create who we are in the present—stories that are handed down in a myriad of ways, from fake front pages to laugh-till-you-cry stories to photo albums to scrapbooks to hope chests to mementos to videos.

Such stories give us context. They reinforce the idea that we do not live and grow in some sort of relational vacuum. They remind us, like a movie storyboard that depicts important scenes and action, how we've changed, and how the world has changed. They reflect the idea that we have histories that can empower us or enslave us, depending on what we do with them.

If Sally and I are struggling in our marriage, for example, I will sometimes think back to those college years before we were married—when we lived 40 miles apart and essentially had a weekends-only relationship. It's good to remember how, for three long years, I would drive home to Corvallis on Highway 99 with a friend who had a '61 VW bug that had a hand-held defrost system (otherwise known as a towel) and no reverse gear. It's good to remember how I would stop at my parents' house, drop off my laundry, and run up the street to see Sally, who lived just around the bend. It's good to remember how hard it was to say good-bye to her on Sunday nights, and how we desperately wished that someday we might always be together.

To remember overcoming that difficulty of time and distance helps us overcome whatever obstacle we face now. It reminds us how much we have invested in our relationship. And how much we have to lose.

Sally and I kept a "memory book" in those days—a book that chronicled our relationship. It now sits on a shelf surrounded by 35 photo albums, which are mainly pictures of our children—the most notable legacy of our perseverance. We also have about a dozen slide trays and, like many folks, enough videotape and Super-8 film to stretch from earth to

Jupiter and back. Not to mention two detailed journals of the boys growing up.

On the days we discovered Sally was pregnant with each of our two sons, I began recording the boys' histories in the form of written journals. At the time, I'm not sure my motives were particularly profound; I just knew that my mother had presented me with a scrapbook of my life when I was 13, and I had found it fascinating. So I passed the legacy on to my sons.

I began the journals on a Smith-Corona typewriter whose spellcheck system involved something called White Out. Now I use a Pentium computer, which repairs most of my spelling wrecks, but not all of them.

While I was writing the entries—anywhere from a handful to a few dozen per year—I sometimes doubted their value. I can remember thinking: *Why am I spending so much time recording the seemingly ordinary events of these guys' lives?* But nearly two decades later, I understand why. I realize that time transforms the ordinary into the extraordinary. Or perhaps it's always been extraordinary, but I lacked the perspective to see it as such.

Like a billboard-size photograph, the image up close looks like nothing more than a random collection of dots. But from a distance, we see the big picture. We see that every one of those dots is there for a reason and, collectively, they tell a story.

> *You're now Age 1, Ryan. When you're a teenager, the '80s will seem ancient. You'll hear me say things like "I remember a time before there were any computers." To me, however, the '80s seem terribly modern. When I was a school boy, you see, the space-age future was the '80s. Now here it is.*

I wrote of "firsts"—for example, the first Christmas tree Ryan helped us cut near Three Creeks Lake. I wrote of what was going on in the world, how movies cost three dollars, and how American hostages in Iran were released on the same day his cousin Carrie was born in 1981. I chronicled that he was playing golf at age two—he's now the No. 1 man on his college team—and chronicled a special moment while we played one-on-one football, just as my father used to play with me.

> *Ry, I remember kicking off to you and the moment froze in my memory: As the ball spiraled down, you had this smile on your face that suggested there was nothing in this world you'd rather be doing than playing football in your backyard. Keep smiling, son. Life's simple pleasures are usually life's best pleasures.*

I recorded my hopes and dreams for my sons. Also some of my fears. "It's good to see you turn 3," I wrote to Jason, "though I must admit it worries me to see you grow older."

I recorded the wins and losses, like the time Jason, as a third-grader, tried out for a fourth-grade baseball team and was told he could not play on it.

> *You were crushed. I have never seen you cry so long and hard. We had bought you a pair of new white baseball shoes. After grieving for a day or two, you said, "Dad, I've decided that I'm not going to wear my new shoes until next season."*

I recorded some frustration:

> *Jason, you are terrible at picking up after yourself. You can see, from Row 32 in the end zone, who threw the key block to spring Derek Loville on a 50-yard touchdown run but can't see a dirty sock that's three feet in front of you.*

I recorded those unforgettable one-liners, like the time Ry was going to the bathroom and yelled, "Dad, look! I made

South America with bubbles!" The time Jason announced to a friend that my spiritual gift was "extortion." And that, according to Jason, the gifts the wise men gave the baby Jesus were "gold, frankencider, and that mold stuff."

I listed what kind of football helmets each of the boys had me paint for them from 1985-1992. And the night I heard Ryan, then 12, and Jason, then 10, jabbering well after they should have been asleep.

> *With a grim face, I marched upstairs. The talking, I realized, was coming from your bedroom, Ry. I peeked in. There you two were, your new Bible open, you giving Jason verses and Jason looking them up. If you're looking for a way to be able to stay up all night, that's it.*

Months flew by. Years flew by. I charted Jason's growing up and, in the excerpts to follow, Ryan's steps to age 18.

> *High school. Unbelievable. My kid, my skinny little kid who, just moments ago, was stuffing his mother's purse down the toilet as a 2-year-old, is in high school. How did you get to be so old?...*
>
> *No, it can't be. It can't be that Ryan Welch has a learner's permit....*
>
> *You're just a shade shorter than mom, having grown almost six inches since last summer....*

The night he went to his first prom. (I had to talk him out of taking his date to the driving range before the dance to hit golf balls.) The play-off basketball game his team lost when the timekeeper gave the opposing team about six seconds to play two "official" seconds. (Not, of course, that I'm still bitter.) Tears for his dead grandfather. ("Dad, I don't want to lose you like you lost Grandpa.")

And finally, the night before his eighteenth birthday, a final page that began: "Dear Ryan: This is it, buddy: My last entry...."

You have come so far. From the seventh man on the JV golf team to the two-time varsity MVP who makes it to state, beats a kid who has a full ride to Arizona State and shoots 84 at night with a glow-in-the-dark ball. From a little kid with glasses and braces, to a handsome, strong, confident young man. From a spiritual baby to someone who, like all of us, is still learning, but is growing in God's grace. You even clean your room once in a while.

I'm proud of you. You inspire me. Now, as someone else once said: Go dream dreams so big that they are sure to fail unless God intervenes. And along the way, remember that you are not alone.

I gave it to Ry the next day. He read it in an evening, walked into my office, and hugged me—a gift more splendid than gold, frankencider, and that mold stuff.

Of Glory and Grace

If a tree has assurance that it can grow to a large size, then there is an advantage for it to invest its energies in growth, because large trees have access to the most sunlight.

—*The Trees in My Forest*

In October 1998, a small college in Oregon—a college with fewer students than some high schools—broke a football record that had stood for 66 years and had been held by two of the country's most esteemed institutions: Notre Dame and Harvard. Linfield College clinched the school's forty-third consecutive winning season—a longer streak than any of the nearly 700 schools on any collegiate level had ever established.

Each year since 1956, the McMinnville school has had more wins in a season than losses. The streak has spanned nine presidents, two wars, and parts of five decades. It began before NASA was founded, before desktop computers and artificial turf were invented, and before some of the *parents* of the current team were even born.

To put the accomplishment in perspective, realize that Harvard's 42-year streak began in 1881, only two decades after the start of the Civil War, and stretched to 1923; Notre

Dame's ran from 1889 to three years after the stock market crash of '29. So you can understand why the Linfield students felt compelled to rip down the goalposts when the record was broken.

Selfishly, I would like to believe the record was established because the current coach, Jay Locey, is a close friend of mine and was the best man at my wedding. I would like to believe it was established because I so inspired Locey with my athletic prowess when we played Little League baseball together or because I taught him the "Gambler's Bet" offense in a dice football game when we were in high school or because I dragged him on high-lake backpacking trips that taught him tenacity (not to mention "never spit with mosquito netting over your face") when we were in college.

But I think the streak really was established because of the strength of a legacy. Oh sure, it had something to do with coaches who could coach and players who could play. It had to do with *X*'s and *O*'s, a fumbled ball that bounced right when it could have bounced left, a favorable ref's call here and there, a blue-chip recruit who might have gone to another school but hated their uniforms, perhaps even fans who, on occasion, helped rally Linfield teams from what looked like certain defeat. But more than anything, I believe it was established because of the four coaches who started and continued that legacy.

Each of them had his own style; clones they were not. But each carried themselves as if the school, the program, the legacy were more important than themselves. Above all, they all instilled two important principles in the players who played for them: First, that the players were *expected* to win. And second, that they were valued highly even if they didn't. In other words, their worth was not dependent on what they accomplished.

I realize those are rather bold deductions for a guy who's outside looking in, and a bit on the touchy-feely side for a sport that's based on knocking one's opponent on his backside. But I base them on research done for a story I once wrote about Linfield football, on what I know of my friend Mr. Locey, and on what Scripture says about the nature of God, the Author of all goodness.

Some young people today are being raised by parents who place high expectations on their children, but whose love for those children is conditional. Such parents leave legacies in their children of high achievement and low self-esteem. Their children accomplish much, but never enough.

Other young people are being raised by parents who love their children, win or lose, but expect so little from them that their kids have no inspiration to become all they were meant to be. Such parents leave legacies in their children of unrealized growth.

If I understand God's Word correctly, the right approach is a third scenario: expecting much *and* forgiving much. Glory and grace, if you will.

One of the most consistent themes in Scripture is that God desperately wants us to be more than we are. Not so we can "win" in the human sense, but so we can glorify the One who gave us life. And that's our purpose for living: to glorify Him, whether it's through raising a child, painting the Sistine Chapel, or passing a football.

In reading God's Word, I do not see the author of dos and don'ts. I see the Author of expectations—expectations designed not to frustrate us through some unreachable quest for perfection, but to encourage us to reflect His glory to the world.

Today, while driving across Oregon's Coast Range, I saw a tree so ablaze with autumn that it looked like a multicolored Popsicle. It was so vibrant that, at first glance, I didn't think it was real. Looking back, I realize that it may never have been *more* real. This was its deepest expression of its being, the height of its glory, nature bringing forth its best.

Likewise, God designed us to be so fully involved in living the "abundant life" that, at times, we should look like that tree. But He doesn't abandon us when we don't. Though He wants us to be vibrant, He loves us no less when we're leafless limbs on a winter's day. He forgives us for not being perfect. In short, He grants us grace.

In his book *What's So Amazing About Grace?* author Philip Yancey says that of all the religions, only Christianity "dares to make God's love unconditional." We cannot work hard enough to earn His favor; we cannot fail badly enough to lose it. "For it is by grace you have been saved, through faith—and this not from yourselves, it is the gift of God—not by works, so that no one can boast" (Ephesians 2:8,9).

Without putting Locey and his predecessors on some divine pedestal, I believe what they've done with their players is to expect much and to forgive much. That's not customary in sports. In the NFL, much is expected and little forgiven; it's not uncommon for the guy who misses the would-be game-winning field goal on Sunday to be released from the team on Monday. And sadly, that kind of cutthroat attitude is frighteningly real even on youth sports levels. I've seen it in my 12 years of coaching baseball, and I saw it recently in a TV investigative report in which a coach—knowing full well he was on camera—angrily chastises his son for striking out, then warns him he'll pay the price when he gets home.

That kind of attitude doesn't wash at Linfield. This is not a machine; as Ad Rutschman, who kept the streak alive as coach from 1968 to 1991, says: "I see our program as one giant classroom." Coaches don't see themselves as gods; in fact, humility has been a trademark of all four men. And the young men who play football at Linfield are not seen as players, but simply as people.

"In theory, all college coaches talk about teaching values," said Mike Riley, a former Linfield assistant and now head coach of the NFL's San Diego Chargers. "But at Linfield it's actually done."

The expectations of excellence and an allowance to fail—therein lie the values of the Linfield legacy. Would that we, as parents, could leave such a legacy with our children: the realization that they are part of something ongoing, something significant that existed long before they arrived and will exist long after they've left, but right now, is depending on them to carry on.

I've read about young gang members who defend their life of violence and self-destruction by saying, "Why not? I don't have anything to lose." They feel so detached from anything or anybody that life becomes cheap. To lose it, then, is to lose nothing; to take someone else's life, then, is to take nothing. But a Linfield player takes the field knowing there's much to lose: pride, a game, the continuation of a legacy. And when there's something to lose, there's motivation to win.

When Linfield has fallen behind, both in games and in seasons, they have an incredible record for rallying. What that suggests is players who have more than speed, strength, and finesse; players who have character, perseverance, and the will to overcome; players and coaches who, when their backs are to the wall, keep cool and trust each other instead of panicking and blaming each other.

In 1987, Linfield began the season 1-4 and had lost games by 24, 21, and 18 points; one more loss in the next four games and the winning-record streak—at the time, 33 years—would be over. One rainy practice, Rutschman, brooding along the sidelines in his rain suit and rubber boots, couldn't watch another dropped pass or botched hand-off. He slammed down his clipboard (even nice guys get peeved occasionally) and ordered the team to the locker room.

"He never once called us losers or said he was ashamed of us," said offensive guard Joe Brim. "He just told us that we weren't being all we should be. That's the thing with Rutschman: He just wanted us to get the most out of ourselves."

He expected more from them because he knew they had more to give. And he got it. Linfield proceeded to win its next three games by an average of 20 points to go 4-4, then rallied in the second half of its final game to clinch yet another winning season.

In 1990, a former Linfield player, Jim Winston, found himself facing long odds himself. He had been paralyzed in a car accident. As he lay in a Los Angeles hospital, what he found himself thinking back to was the undefeated national championship Linfield football team he had played on, and to Rutschman. He remembered how the coach, on the eve of a game, would say something like, "Tomorrow, gentlemen, you will face adversity every single play. How you react to that adversity will determine who wins. It will be that way tomorrow, five years from now—every single day of your life."

Within days of Winston's accident, Rutschman was on the phone to his former defensive tackle, encouraging him not to quit. "I've never forgotten how he told the team that self-pity leads to self-destruction," said Winston.

Since then, Winston has gotten married, works in television, and still feels part of the Linfield legacy. "Here I am, paralyzed, and yet I still feel like I did when I was so strong and fast and playing for Rutschman. I still feel like a winner."

Teams with character reach deep when they must; so do young people whose battles are waged well beyond the chalked lines of a football field—young people who are encouraged to soar but are loved even when they don't.

Keeper of the Woods

Exploited forests will not and cannot renew themselves, given modern methods of forest exploitation....Wood is a renewable resource. Forests, in their original, pristine form, are not.

—*The World of Northern Evergreens*

Here I am, Pop, back in the same country cemetery outside Carlton, Oregon, where we said good-bye to you ten years ago.

I remember the service on that cool afternoon. I remember returning to the city and writing a column about you for the newspaper where I worked. I wrote about how you were a vanishing breed. A man who held one job his entire life: farmer. A man who was married to the same woman for 60 years. A man who died in the same farmhouse where he had been born 89 years earlier.

After the column was published, lots of people wrote and called to say what a wonderful man you must have been. And how they knew a Pop of their own. But I'm afraid you wouldn't get the same warm reaction were I to write that same column today. America isn't the same country it was even ten years ago.

Much has changed, Pop. Too much.

You're not going to understand this, but you would be considered, well, "politically incorrect" these days.

I remember a man who remained faithful to his wife, taught his children right from wrong, and kept his family together despite drought and Depression. But today, Pop, amid my baby-boom generation, you would be guilty of promoting "family values," whose proponents, Hugh Downs once told his "20/20" TV audience, are fueled by the same intolerance that fueled Hitler and the Ku Klux Klan.

I remember a man who got tears in his eyes when singing "Amazing Grace" at Grace Baptist Church which he helped found in Carlton. But today, Pop, you would be considered a fool for worshiping some obsolete God when you could be searching for your inner child, winning by intimidation, or awakening the warrior spirit within.

I remember a man who made his grandchildren wind chimes for Christmas and helped other farmers bale their hay when storms were coming. I remember a man who insisted that we all hold hands before a meal and, when he had finished praying, would give the hands he was holding an encouraging squeeze. But today, Pop, you would be cast as a cultural villain, a white European male who wears a fur-lined cap and eats meat loaf.

As I said, the country has changed in the ten years since you died. Oh, some of it's been for the better. If not overcoming our prejudices, we're at least confronting some of them, especially against women and minorities. Recycling has caught on. And the Big Hunk folks finally made a wrapper that doesn't stick to the candy bar.

But evil, if possible, has gotten more evil. A bomb blew up in a federal building in Oklahoma City, killing 168 people. A mother in South Carolina drowned her two sons so they wouldn't interfere with her relationship with her boyfriend. And this morning's paper told of a St. Louis teacher who died after being punched by a fourth-grader who didn't like his homework assignment.

What's going on, Pop?

Crack cocaine. Drive-by shootings. Assisted suicide. Partial-birth abortions. Video poker. Trashy talk shows. Greedy athletes. Computer pornography. Runaway lawsuits. Shock radio. Domestic violence. Political lies. All have mushroomed in the last decade.

In many cases, the abnormal has become normal; right and wrong have traded places. In 1992, the vice president of the United States suggested it would be better for children to be raised by two parents than by one. He was verbally lynched. A year earlier, ex-basketball player Magic Johnson revealed he was HIV-positive after admitting to having had sex with hundreds of women. He was hailed as a hero who had been dealt an unfair hand.

In Oregon, your great-granddaughters can't even have their ears pierced without having a parent or guardian present. But they can legally have an abortion without even *notifying* a parent or guardian, much less having them present.

It's as if the same baby-boom generation that understands so well the interconnectedness of links in the environmental chain ignores the connections in the moral chain. The same generation that straps itself to trees to prevent clear-cutting of old-growth forests seems intent on clear cutting stands of old-growth values—values that aren't good because of their longevity, but because they're God-given and people-proven.

I'm the first to admit that some selective thinning is in order. This isn't about one side being right and the other being wrong, but about how America is fast turning into a ridge of stumps.

Meanwhile, the canyon between groups of people has gotten deeper and wider. From the vicious anti-Christian remarks of *Time* magazine's "Man of the Year," Ted Turner, to the Darwin car symbols that ridicule the religious "fish" symbol, Christians like you, Pop, remain fair game for mocking—this in a time when we're supposedly trying to celebrate our differences as people.

Then again, some people, in the name of Christ, do their share to widen that gap. They wrongly claim God hates homosexuals or they take deadly revenge on abortion doctors or they subtly boast of their faith with a fish-eating-the-Darwin-symbol symbol. They act more like the Pharisee of Luke 18:11, who said, "God, I thank you that I am not like other men—robbers, evildoers, adulterers..." than like the repentant tax collector who said, "God, have mercy on me, a sinner."

What we've lost in this country, Pop, is trust. We don't trust each other. We don't trust our government. We don't trust God. What we trust in, Pop, is ourselves, which you once said was a little like standing beneath a lone tree in a field during a lightning storm.

Gram once told me the story about the toothless old man who showed up asking you for free hay. You gladly obliged, she said, only to find out later that the man had money to pay the two farmers down the road for their hay. You trusted people...perhaps too much. But today, trust is the rarest of virtues, mirrored in broken promises of spouses, lying politicians, even the head of United Way, who was recently convicted of embezzling from the very charity he directed.

We've become like a bunch of Herefords caught in quicksand: The harder we struggle on our own, the deeper we sink. So where is the hope that we can free ourselves, Pop?

Maybe it's in taking a step back so we can see the forest for the trees. Maybe it's in our willingness to stop clear-cutting America's old-growth value system long enough to assess the damage we've done. Maybe it's in a reforestation effort that acknowledges the One who understands—better than we fallible humans—the ways of the woods.

Well, it's getting late; I need to go. But I want you to know one last thing, Pop: Every now and then, one of your great-grandsons, while playing baseball out back, will rip a line drive smack into the wind chime you made us. And it'll jolt me, as if to say: *Don't forget, don't forget*.

I haven't forgotten, Pop. I can still hear your soft, farm-drawl voice. And I can still feel your calloused hand squeeze mine after a meal-time prayer, as if passing on hope to a generation in need of it.

Fathers and Sons

> Every child is entranced by the maple tree's winged seed pod. Its graceful acrobatics have a vital purpose, however, spinning the seed far from the parent tree in search of the sunlight and rich soil essential for its survival.
>
> —*North American Trees*

Any moment now, I'm thinking, I'm going to hear the sound of his squishy tennis shoes coming down the dock behind me. He'll be carrying a grocery sack full of food and a couple packets of two-pound-test, tapered fly leader from the lodge store—just enough food to get us through the next week of camping on the far end of the lake. He'll be smoking that pipe of his. He'll be wearing an undershirt, light blue jeans, and cheap sunglasses that will probably wind up on the bottom of the lake before the week is out. His tennis shoes will be wet because when we go camping, he is forever shoving off the boat or beaching the boat or standing in the shallows, fishing.

"Wanna drive?" he'll ask.

I always wanna drive. I am 15 years old. We hop in the 14-foot Dillabaugh that my father built himself, I give the Johnson 35 a crank, and we're off. Instinctively, I point the bow toward the nub of Irish Mountain, as he taught me to do, and we head for camp.

"Can I help you?" says the voice.

"What's that?" I ask.

"Can I get something for you?"

"Uh, no, I just came to look at the lake," I say.

The store owner wakes me from my wanderings. I am not 15 years old. I am 44. It is late September, and I am standing in the lodge at Cultus Lake, on the eastern flank of Oregon's Cascade Mountains, lost in another time. I am looking at the mountain and docks and water so clear that I used to hang my head over the side of a pram and, wearing a diving mask, pretend I was hunting for sunken treasure, the remains of those famous shipwrecks: the Nehi, the Heidelberg, the Bubble-Up....

"I used to come here long ago," I tell the woman.

"Has it changed?"

"Doesn't quite smell the same in the lodge. I thought it might."

"We just bought it last year. Put in new stools in the restaurant. Gettin' ready to close up for the winter. Cabins are already closed."

She and a friend are sitting in a corner, watching Saturday-morning cartoons, smoking. It doesn't seem right. It doesn't seem right that there's a TV now in the pine-paneled lodge, and it doesn't smell the same, and there are no Archie comic books in the racks. It doesn't seem right that it's cold and windy outside and nobody is out on the lake. But mostly what doesn't seem right is that he's not here.

My dad.

Only twice have I been to this lake without him. Why can't I seem to forget the guy? He's been gone two years now. He wasn't my hero. He wasn't Superdad. We were always hounding him to quit smoking. Chances are, we would have hiked to Muskrat Lake or one of the Teddy

Lakes that evening to go fly-fishing, and if the bug hatch were light and no trout were feeding on the surface, we would have kept fishing...and fishing...and fishing, as if my father were more interested in the results than the father-son experience. Spiritually, he and I differed. In high school, I came to believe that God was personal and wanted a relationship with all His creations; my father believed God was someone you called on only in dire emergencies, and in the meantime, was best used in fishing jokes.

And yet something draws me back to the man and places like this, and I find it so easy to forgive him—perhaps because he so easily forgave me. My remembrances of him are like a football highlight film: The botched plays get edited out before the memory reel begins.

I hear him telling me I need to buckle up. I see him sitting in a lawn chair, cheering when one of his grandsons steps into the batter's box. I remember being a boy and how the last thing I heard at night before falling asleep was my dad going around the house turning off the lights and locking all the doors, and how safe that made me feel. And how my sister and I were the only kids around with 16 mm home movies with music and titles, because our father was a professional photographer. And how when I was really small, while he was napping sideways on the couch, I would snuggle in that nook behind his bent legs as if it were my secret fort. And how when I grew up, he didn't demand that I be *him* all over again and take over his business, go to Oregon State, and become a Sigma Alpha Epsilon.

Maybe that's why I'm here: just because I want to remember him—both when he was young and when he had grown old, like the year before he died when I drove him to Portland to pick up Mom from the airport. "Dad," I said after we had gone just a few blocks, "you need to buckle up." It was like that late fall day when you notice the wind is cold and first realize winter is coming.

Maybe it's because I am the man's legacy. Sometimes I see a photo of myself at a distance and think: *I look just like the guy—squatty legs and all.* Or I can't find my keys and think: *Just like my dad.* But mostly, I'm proud to be his son. My mother inspired me to write. She has always been curious about people, places, ideas, and events—and curiosity to a writer is like flour to a baker. But my father's father was a fine artist, as was my dad before he shifted to photography. Somehow, some of those artistic genes sifted down to me, though I create my images with words instead of photographs or drawings. I think he taught me to appreciate humor, to not follow a crowd, to improvise and invent. And I appreciate him for that.

Maybe it's because I'm learning that death doesn't really end your relationship with someone; it only alters it.

Maybe it's because parents and children are connected in some sort of deeper way, almost like salmon are connected to their headwaters, and will fight through torrential currents to return. As Jane Kirkpatrick writes in her novel *Mystic Sweet Communion*:

> We are all in first relation to our parents, first attached to them. Without them there's an emptiness, a missing linkage, with no time after they are gone to discover them: what our parents thought of when they fell in love or took on a new adventure. No time now to ask them, to see how we are like them or how different as we've moved inside the circles of our making. No more time to tell them how we loved them.

Maybe it's because, as sons, we have this burden to make our fathers proud, even after they're gone. When at age 12 I first drove our boat the three-mile length of Cultus Lake by myself, I sensed I had made my father proud. But I didn't fully understand the power of father-son pride until recently, after watching my own son play in a qualifying event for a

PGA Nike golf tournament. At 19 and 5-foot-8, he was the youngest and smallest of 115 entrants, and one of the few amateurs. He had played hard and smart but hadn't been able to sink a putt all day.

But he had handled himself with honor and dignity, and battled to the end on a golf course whose tees were set as far back as possible, and whose pins were tucked deep behind traps. That night, after he had returned to college, I e-mailed him to tell him I was proud of him.

His return message said,

> Thanks for the note. And thanks for coming today. My favorite part about playing well is when you are there to see me do things right. I loved hitting approach shots close and then getting the "fist-pump" from you. I want so badly to play well for you—I want you to be able to see me putt like I know I can. But it fills me with joy to hear you say that you're proud of me. As much as an 81 hurts, I'd take an "I'm proud of you" over a 71 any day.

Maybe it's all this and more: the mountains and driving by Sparks Lake, where my father's father camped with my dad in the thirties, and where I've camped with my two sons. And that here in Central Oregon is where my journey as a father began, where Sally and I took our sons home from the hospital.

It was here, in December 1979, that I wrote the only poem I ever wrote for my father. It was just prior to Ryan's first Christmas. I called it "Fathers and Sons":

> On a December night, not long ago
> That grandson of yours had a fright
> So a bottle I warmed
> In the wee hours of morn
> And flicked on the Christmas tree lights

The wind outside, it bothered him not
So trustful the look in his eyes
While the fire burned low
My mind took a stroll
To a time when I was like Ry

Treading back nearly twenty-five years
when I was the 6-month-old lad
You were the one
Who cradled his son
And, perhaps, remembered your dad

It's a special bond, not often felt
Between a father and his boy
And it makes me feel proud
That I've been allowed
To drink from this cup of joy

Someday, perhaps, that grandson of yours
Who's now fast asleep as I write
Will cradle the one
He knows as his son
And think of his dad in the night

And if, on that night, the thoughts he recalls
Are like those I recall of you
Then in that December
My son will remember
A warm, loving father, too.

I found the poem in a cedar chest in my father's office on the night after he died. It isn't exactly Robert Frost, but I'm glad I wrote it. I'm glad he read it. I'm glad that he saved it in that cedar chest and that it was there for me to find.

Now I stand on a dock and the past blows at me like the wind whipping across the lake. It chills me with the reality of years gone by, making me feel wistful and a bit old. At the same time, it invigorates me, making me thankful I had something good enough to miss once it was gone.

Like our vacations to Cultus Lake back in the sixties, memories are not always perfect. Sometimes they are downright painful, because we find ourselves remembering not only what was, but what might have been.

In our camping days, my father used to encourage us to leave a campsite neater than we found it, and I think that applies to our lives as well. We can lament that the campsite wasn't perfect, or we can accept that, though we have no control over its condition when we arrive, we do have control over how it is left.

Before leaving Cultus Lake on this late September morning, I've already thought about coming back, perhaps this next time with the sailboat my father left to Mom and will ultimately be left to me. I'll come in the fall after the crowds have gone but before the snow flies. I'll crank up the motor. And instinctively, I'll point the boat to the nub of Irish Mountain, as he taught me to do, and head for camp.

A Legacy of My Own

> No matter how a tree is pruned, it always has a form of its own that it "wants" to keep and will return to, come what may. The pruner must find that form and work with, rather than against, it, or he or she will always be at war with the tree.
>
> —*Bringing a Garden to Life*

I.

When Jason was born in 1982, my wife and I bought a new digital alarm clock. Frankly, I'm not sure what the relationship was between these two seemingly incongruent events, but I do know this: Every day for 16 years, that clock worked faithfully, telling me the time, waking me up and giving me that extra ten-minute snooze-alarm period that I used like a sleep junky, first disciplining myself to allow only one ten-minute extra snooze, then rationalizing that a second couldn't hurt, and ultimately degenerating to the point where I would sleep most of the night in ten-minute increments.

But soon after Jason turned 16, the alarm went off one morning and the digital numbers did a strange thing: they started flashing off and on and changing incredibly fast, like time-lapse photography. The digits would go from 7:30 A.M. to 8 A.M. in a matter of minutes. The only way I could reset the clock was to unplug it and plug it back in.

Somewhat like in the movie *Groundhog Day* in which a man's life repeats itself over and over, this oddity continued day after day. For most people, this would mean it's time to buy a new alarm clock. For me, it was a clear premonition that now that my son was 16, life was going to go past incredibly fast, and no pressing of that snooze-alarm button could allow me to put off its inevitable march.

It was a sign that I would soon have to start going through all the letting go that I had just gone through with my first son, only this one would have added poignancy, like opening your last present under the tree. One day Jason will be there, as he will have been for the past 18 years. And then, zing, just like that, he'll be gone; our last arrow, disappearing in the sky.

More than that, it was a sign that I had better contemplate the future, which is not as easy or as comfortable as contemplating the past. I've always been one to record my experiences, to contemplate what's happened in my life. So why is it so hard to consider what may happen once I'm gone? Why is it so hard to consider the legacy I will leave my sons?

Perhaps because the future can be—as Ryan said about leaving for college—*kinda scary*. When I see an old man walking, hunched over, I sometimes wonder: Will that be me someday? Naw, I could never be that old. Then I wonder: Did that man, at age 44, see an old man walking, hunched over, and think the same thought? If so, the man was wrong. Which means I could be, too.

Perhaps because contemplating the legacies you've inherited—even if some aren't quite what you would wish for—is less risky than contemplating the legacies you'll leave. Despite its foibles and frustrations, the past is as permanent as the fully developed prints I used to make in my father's photo darkroom; I may not have liked everything I saw, but it was a fixed record that I could at least deal with or discard. The future, on the other hand, is like the photograph still in the developer, the image still very much in flux. And the unknown carries with it a sense of angst; you never know just when that image is going to be completed or, when it is, whether you're going to like what you see.

Life changes fast. I look at a picture of Ryan and Jason, then 13 and 10, standing in front of a birch tree on the day we planted it: Halloween Day 1992. Twelve feet tall with a trunk about an inch thick, the tree is now about 35 feet tall with an eight-inch trunk. In the photo, the boys look as spindly as the tree; not anymore.

They never remember a time before touch-tone phones. To them, stamps have always cost 32 or 33 cents. They've never seen an eight-track tape. They don't understand the expression "you sound like a broken record." They've never written a school paper on a typewriter. All this, in just one generation. Which raises the threat that if *things* can become obsolete, well, so can people. So can *I*.

When I took Jason to his first major-league baseball game in 1989, Ken Griffey Jr. stepped to the plate for his first major-league at-bat in the colossal Kingdome and promptly hit a home run. Ten years later, Griffey is still hitting home runs, but the Kingdome will soon be torn down; it is, at age 22, considered obsolete.

It's hard imagining that your Pentium computer will someday be sold at an antique fair to someone who finds it "quaint" and will perhaps incorporate it into a dried-flower arrangement. It's hard imagining that people in the future may see a Legacy (the kind you drive, not pass on to your children) and say "Must be an old-fashioned car rally going on somewhere."

But what's really hard is imagining that someday I'll probably be only a digitized photograph on some chrome wall of my grandchildren's space villa. And that I'll go unnoticed for months, maybe years, until one of my great-grandson's pals, while munching on a pizza pellet during a break in their virtual-reality football game, says, "So, who's the geezer with the monster earlobes?" And my great-grandson will say, "Let me check," punch some finger commands into his wristwatch computer, and peel off a grocery-receipt-sized printout comprised of data as cold as death: *Bob Welch, b. Feb. 3, 1954; m. Sally Youngberg, Aug. 22, 1975; two children…*

I don't want that. I want that kid to turn to his pal and say, "That's my great-grandfather 'Bob'—weird names back then, huh?"—and tell him a story about who I was. I don't even care if it's the story about me getting my mouth stuck open in the dentist's office. I want him to know me as something more than a thumbnail sketch, a data entry on the family tree, a birth date and death date.

Better yet, I want that kid to be different—if even in some small way—because I once lived. I understand the dust-to-dust stuff in Ecclesiastes. I understand the brevity of life and how, in a universe that scientists estimate has 100 billion stars alone, I'm fairly small potatoes. But if Clarence, the angel from *It's a Wonderful Life,* were showing me what life would be like if I had never lived, I would want to see that some people turned out differently because of me.

Sounds egotistical, I know, but I don't think it is. Unlike George Bailey, I wouldn't need to be responsible for having saved the lives of every soldier on a transport ship because I had earlier saved a sibling from drowning. But I admit it: I would want to have made a difference. I wouldn't want to have been on that snowy bridge, thinking about jumping because I figured I was worth more dead than alive.

Reality is, I want to be worth something while dead *and* alive. My prayer is George Bailey's prayer at the end of the movie, after he's seen what life would have been like without him, and he's back at that same bridge: *I want to live again. Please, God, let me live again.*

Let me live again not only in the heavenly sense, but in the sense that part of what I model or teach or stand for gets lived out in the lives of my sons, both while I'm here and after I'm gone.

It still smacks of egotism, considering ourselves as legacy-givers. But that's only if you believe your legacy should be to produce a clone or clones of yourself, which isn't the idea. Like trees, God made each of us different. No two of us are expected to even grow at the same rate. It's my job to help my children become all He made them to be, not all I *think* they should be.

May my sons be rooted in Him, but free to be the unique creations He designed them to be, free to follow their personal bents, free to even fail on occasion.

Frankly, if my sons are aiming to be like me, they're aiming too low. I want them to aspire to be like their heavenly Father, not their earthly father; aspire to His will, not mine. If I can reflect His love through how I live, and my sons seek to emulate that, wonderful. But it's better that my sons pattern their lives after the original model than the flawed replica that is me.

If you're trying to cut six pieces of wood the same size and shape, you can try the Bob Welch School of Carpentry: Cut one piece and use it as the pattern for your next cut, and use the second piece as the pattern for your next cut, and the third piece as the pattern for your next cut, etc. The problem is that the small error you make on each cut compounds itself with each generation, and you wind up with boards that are like your temper at the point when you try to use those boards: short (or, other times, long). Better to measure each cut by the one original pattern than by generation after slightly flawed generation of your own.

Early in my journalism career, I had the privilege of editing the first-ever Sunday edition at the newspaper where I worked. When I scanned through the inaugural issue, I was thrilled—until I realized that in a photo cutline, I had spelled Stanford with an extra *d*—Standford. (It did not help matters that it was a simple word, nor that my boss had attended the university; why couldn't I have misspelled, say, Xavier or Gustavus Adolphus College?)

But life went on. I grew older. My sons grew up. And one day Ryan, then 17, asked if I would edit a story he had written for a class. There it was—a reference in his story to "Standford." I laughed out loud. Not all legacies are honorable; better that our children's authority on spelling be the dictionary and that their authority on life be the Word of God.

II.

Despite our flaws—of which mine range from a propensity to overorchestrate the lives of my wife and sons to an inability to fold road maps—God allows us the privilege of passing on values to a new generation. To model His character. To interpret His Word. In more basic terms, to help our children learn to spell. To that end, I hope the legacy I leave my sons is at least a reasonable facsimile of the legacy He has left for us.

May my sons be men of courage and compassion.

May they love deep and wide, realizing that, as 1 Corinthians 13 points out, without it we are only "clanging cymbals."

May they avoid the snares of self-righteousness, remembering that "whoever humbles himself will be exalted" (Matthew 23:12).

May they trust in their heavenly Father even when the lights go out—*especially* when the lights go out. "The righteous," says Proverbs 12:3, "cannot be uprooted."

May they be quick to see the good in others, slow to anger, fast to forgive.

In a time when some believers live lives in constant fear, as if God were some sort of celestial cop, may my sons avoid the land mines of legalism. Instead, may they embrace the gospel of grace that the Scriptures describe.

May they trust in a God who's not bumper-sticker thin, but whose unconditional love and forgiveness stretches as far as the east is from the west, and who says to the rich man and the ragamuffin alike: "Come to me, all you who are weary and burdened, and I will give you rest" (Matthew 11:28).

May they be men of humility, quick to applaud the triumphs of others, slow to boast of their own.

May they never ever ever *ever* clip their fingernails and leave the remains on the coffee table or drop them between the cushions in the couch.

May they serve rather than be served.

May they live life as the gift that it is. Scripture speaks of living "the abundant life." And yet so many of us sleepwalk our way through it. May they notice God's glory in the vine maple turning red on the McKenzie Pass and appreciate the sweetness of a six-year-old trying to hit that high note in "Away in a Manger" ("The stars in the sky..."), and notice the cool sound of rain trickling down a gutter (especially if they stay in Oregon, since they'll hear that sound often).

May they dare to dream. A friend's father, when my friend was ready to go take on the world, told his son that dreams only disappoint. Fortunately, my friend didn't listen; he listened, instead, to his mother, who never doubted his potential. He went on to become an author, a national speaker on marriage and the family, and the most Christlike pastor I've ever known.

He took his less-than-stellar upbringing and merged it with a woman whose childhood was even more painful; together, through trusting in God, they raised four wonderful children. One drowned at age five; they feel his loss every day. And yet my friend used that loss to steel his faith, to reach out to others who have faced the death of someone near, to learn and grow.

He did not let the loss rob his joy. Instead, he told his other children to not only live, but dream. And to not only dream, but to dream big.

One son recently got married and is working toward his Christian ministries master's degree. Another son recently helped his college soccer team set an all-time NCAA record for number of consecutive games without a loss. And his daughter is studying at the college where she always hoped she could someday attend.

May my sons not only dream big, but laugh long and hard. And, most often, at themselves (or at me, which in our house sort of goes without saying).

May they appreciate the moment, but also remember the past and anticipate the future. This is a legacy from my mother, who occasionally reminds us that we can enjoy an experience in three ways: by looking forward to it, by experiencing it, and by remembering it.

If they're blessed with children, may they have the wisdom to pass on anything honorable that I've passed on to them (something even more significant than the 1995 University of Oregon Rose Bowl shirts I've bought for the grandchildren I don't even have). And may they have the courage to leave behind that which is not honorable, like my occasional temper, my compulsiveness about *doing* rather than *being*, and my propensity to leave Post-Its (the poor man's

Daytimer) everywhere. (Found on the side of my shoe just tonight: *Call Steve Panter.*)

Finally, may they use their time on earth to bring glory to the One who gave them their time on earth. Time, whether it's reflected in the changing of seasons or stiffness in the joints or haywire clock radios in which hours seemingly become minutes, *is* of the essence.

May my sons use it wisely, remembering that each day they're building legacies of their own. And that someday it will be their photos on the wall that some great-grandchild looks up and sees.

May that little boy or girl be different, if even in some small way, because my sons once lived.

Losing Leaves

The Coming of Winter

> Leaves of forest trees can be said to be the planet's most important producers of organic material, since more than four-fifths of all plant tissue is contained in trees. For all their importance, leaves are temporary fixtures.
>
> —*Forest*

Until 1996, I thought I was immortal. Well, sort of. I looked at death like I looked at a dental appointment made six months in advance: something that, intellectually, I could admit would someday occur but was so far in the future that I could easily rationalize it would never *really* happen.

I turned 40 and didn't think about my death. I watched my friends turn 40 and didn't think about my death. Then my father died and I started thinking about my death. Not in a compulsive sort of way. Not even in a fearful sort of way. But in an almost practical way, as if seeing, for the first time, how the cycle works.

Losing a parent, in this case a father, is the last line of defense between the living and the dead. In my case, that's because even if I didn't have a perfect relationship with the guy, I assumed he was immortal because—well, because fathers aren't supposed to die. In my mind, my father was always about 35 years old. He was helping me build a pinewood derby race car or pointing out Sputnik to me and my sister in the sky above Draper Court or standing in front of our Impala one night at the beach, striking wacky poses while Mom, the self-appointed lights technician, flashed the brights on and off to create that monster-like flicker effect.

"He's gone." In the summer of 1996, those are the two words my sister used over the phone in telling me that my father had died. Six months later, two other words further reminded me that there's a finish line out there somewhere.

"Skin cancer."

In a routine physical, my doctor had found a spot high on my cheekbone, near my ear. He scraped a sample of it. I never, for an instant, assumed he would find what he thought he might find. Cancer, even less serious forms such as non-melanoma skin cancer, was for old people, distant relatives, and those "how-you-can-prevent" articles in *Reader's Digest*.

I remember calling the doctor's office to hear the results. I had a cordless phone and was simultaneously unpacking from a trip to the beach while I called; that's how nonchalant I was.

"The results were positive," the nurse said. "You do have skin cancer."

I did not gasp. I did not go numb. Instead, I remember feeling humbled, as if I had lived my whole life thinking I was somehow in control, and God was reminding me that I was mistaken. True, He grants us free will; I can choose to live my life as I choose. But when it comes to death, we are like the little kids on those boats at Disneyland: We may *think* we're steering, but under the water, where we cannot see, the boat follows the rails.

Two surgeries later, the cancer—a relatively tame, slow-spreading variety—was removed. But I am not the same. Slowly, I'm realizing that I'm going to die. Maybe today.

Maybe 50 years from now. But I'm going to die. Someday, my sons are going to get phone calls and someone is going to say, "He's gone."

Two days ago, a friend and coworker—and a guy who ran on the same Hood-to-Coast team with me—walked into my office to say good-bye. He was leaving the next day to do a story in Rwanda, a country torn by civil war and a fairly dangerous place to be because of its volatility. We hugged, then he handed me an envelope. "Give this to my wife if anything should happen to me," he said.

It was an envelope full of letters to his wife and three children. Though he had spent a lifetime investing deeply in them all, he wanted to leave a reminder of his love for them, just in case he never had another chance. After he left, it occurred to me that we would all do well to live like that: to always make sure that we've left those we love something that reminds them of that love, just in case we never have another chance.

I'm reminded of death each day as I look at the obituaries. They used to be of people who served in World War II and belonged to the Elks and had a zillion grandchildren. Now they're sprinkled heavily with people my own age—people who served in Vietnam and belonged to tennis clubs and didn't have grandchildren.

But when I look at God's ways, I'm reminded of something else: Only in death can our ultimate legacy be left. "I tell you the truth," says Jesus in John 12:24, "unless a kernel of wheat falls to the ground and dies, it remains only a single seed. But if it dies, it produces many seeds."

Our culture generally teaches death as an ending, but in many ways it's a beginning. Because death brings our legacies to complete fruition. After I wrote *A Father for All Seasons,* a man who read it wrote this to me: "I used to think my father was a fairly insignificant guy in my life. Then he died, and it was like, for the first time, I realized all he had given to me."

It's not until a tree dies and its growth rings are examined that the biologist can truly understand its history. Likewise, it's not until a person dies that his or her legacy is totally revealed.

When I listen to Rich Mullins' songs, I nearly always wonder why God allowed such a talented and faithful troubadour to die so young. And yet just as I'm moved by his music, so am I reminded that his songs go on without him—as do all of our songs.

It's like that postscript on contest commercials: *Need not be present to win*. What we give to the world doesn't require us to stay in this world for it to have an impact.

In the movie, *Mr. Holland's Opus*, an aging music teacher laments losing the job, the school, and the students he so passionately loved. What's more, his career is ending with his never having found time to have a piece of music he's written performed.

Surprise! He walks into the school auditorium and there await his former students, poised with instruments, ready to play his opus. "Look around you," one of the students tells the packed theater. "We are your symphony, Mr. Holland. We are the melodies and the notes of your opus, and we are the music of your life."

The end of his career, he realizes, is not the end of his influence. It goes on without him, transferred to all the students whose lives he touched—students who will transfer some of what they've learned from him to others.

At the end of a life, what matters isn't the person's stock holdings or business titles or committee appointments. What matters is the lives he or she touched. Like sea foam on a wintry Oregon beach, the insignificant stuff blows away in the wind; what remains is the substance of faith, family, and friends.

As I walked "the wall" at Thurston High School after a young gunman had killed two of his classmates and wounded 24 others, I saw symbols of relationships—people-to-people relationships and people-to-God relationships—in letters, poems, crosses, Scripture, and pictures. Symbols of connecting to one another, and connecting to the One who first gave us life. I saw the hope of heaven, thanks for what the deceased had meant to others, and reminders that the lives of the dead live on in the lives of the living.

"You won't be forgotten," said a number of notes.

For those who have gone on before us, the privilege—and obligation—of living with purpose is over. But for those who remain, it is just beginning. Consider the end of Steven Spielberg's gut-wrenchingly real movie based on the Normandy invasion, *Saving Private Ryan*: Captain John Miller (Tom Hanks) lies dying beside the very soldier whose life, in essence, he has saved.

His final words: "Earn this."

The scene fades to present day as a white-haired Private Ryan stands by the grave where lies the soldier who, more than 50 years ago, helped save him. Well behind Ryan stand his wife, children, and four grandchildren—his legacies.

"I didn't invent anything," he says. "I didn't cure any diseases. I worked a farm. I raised a family. I lived a life. I only hope, in your eyes at least, I earned what you did for me."

The scene, one of the most moving I've witnessed on film, reminds us that what we are *now* is often due to what someone else was *then*. The sacrifice Miller made would have been wasted had Ryan squandered the freedom he had been given.

Most of the sacrifices made for us are less gallant than this, and yet can still have a huge impact on us. I am different because of the sacrifices my father made for me. He spent much of his life photographing wild college students at their fraternity and sorority parties—not exactly dream-job stuff—so that I could go to college and not have to do the same; so I could have it better; so I could be more than I would have been otherwise.

Likewise, the world is different because of what our heavenly Father did for us. He allowed His Son to die on a cross so that we could be unshackled from sin; so we could have it better; so we could be more than we would have been otherwise. But the sacrifice is wasted if we squander the freedom He gave us.

Death is painful. Still, it is necessary to bring us—and, in a sense, those who follow—to completeness. In autumn, when deciduous trees paint the landscape with hues of red, yellow, and orange, their glorious colors suggest life at its most brilliant. The transition, however, is triggered by an ironic twist: death. For if leaves did not wither and die each fall, the tree itself would wither and die in the winter. Green leaves would become a liability—thousands of extra mouths to feed in a time when a tree's food supply is at its lowest.

In October, when you fly into an area where the deciduous trees have just lost their leaves, your bird's-eye view reveals halos of gold around such trees. A month later, the same flight will offer no such grandeur; the leaves will be wet and soggy and will have blended into the muted colors of earth.

But just because we cannot see grandeur does not mean it doesn't exist; legacies often work their way through nature and people in ways we'll never see. Those fallen leaves still have purpose, enriching the soil for generations to come, their deaths not in vain.

In death, every part of a tree ultimately restores to the ecosystem the useful organic elements that were locked up in the tree during its lifetime. Death supersedes life and life rises again from what is dead.

A leaf in transition…a soldier at Normandy…God's Son on a cross. When I see the hues of autumn, I'm reminded of what death's most honorable legacy is: life.

The Long Good-bye

Trees receive a most beautiful burial. Nature takes fallen trees gently to her bosom—at rest from storms. They seem to have been called home out of the sky to sleep.

—*John Muir*

My mother watched her father die just down the hall from where she had given birth to me and my sister.

It wasn't anything like she thought it would be. She always thought it would happen like this: Her father would be in his garden behind the house on Colorado Lake Road, digging up bulbs or potting geraniums or picking plums—his transistor radio tuned to Paul Harvey or an Oregon State football game—and his heart would simply stop. After all, the man was nearly 90 years old. It just seemed right that he should die suddenly, without pain. It just seemed right that he should die in his favorite place, the place from which all his earthly blessings flowed, and be united with the wife he had missed so much since her death years ago.

Instead it happened after he spent nearly a decade in a nursing home in which large signs on the walls reminded patients what month it was and hunched-over people in wheelchairs mumbled to people who lived in another time and the smell of urine hung in the air as if to mock the dignity of the aged. It happened after my grandfather had broken a hip and sometimes forgot that his wife was dead and developed arthritis so debilitating he could not hold a spoon. It happened with a nurse dressed up in a Halloween costume checking my grandfather's pulse and saying to my mother, "Your father is gone."

Sometimes we write our own scripts for the future only to find that life can be a ruthless editor. At first, we wonder why. Why can't it be the way we want it to be? Then later, once the curtain closes and the theater is dark and we've had time to think, we perhaps discover that the edited version, though not what we would have chosen, was perfect in its imperfection. We realize, perhaps, that people pass on legacies not only in how they live, but in how they die. We learn that perhaps our script was rejected because we were never meant to write it, but to actually play a part in it—not to watch it from a distance, but to take a supporting role onstage.

So it happened like this: At age 90, my grandfather had a stroke that would require him to have round-the-clock care for the rest of his life. No more driving the Olds past the SAE house to see if the boys were keeping the lawn mowed and apple trees along 30th Street pruned. No more watching Oregon State football games. No more walking on the beach by the cabin he had bought in 1936 for 500 dollars and which had become our family's common ground.

My mother, 62 at the time, worked full-time outside the home; my father, 65, worked part-time in the home. They would find him a suitable foster-care facility, they decided. But then my father, in uncharacteristic boldness, announced that he had invited Grandpa to come live with them. Dad could care for him during the day; Mom in the evening.

The decision dramatically changed their lives, sometimes for the good, sometimes not. They ate lots of sit-down meals together—more than usual. They sat out on the front porch, the three of them, and talked to passersby—something Mom and Dad had never done before. But within the year, "Schu"—that's what everyone called my grandfather because his last name was Schumacher—was having considerable difficulty walking, and my father had developed a heart condition, which hampered his ability to help out.

That forced the hardest decision of my mother's life: to put her father in a nursing home. For six decades, the two of them had enjoyed a solid, though not spectacular, relationship. With roots deep in the military and Methodist church, my grandfather leaned more toward the practical than the emotionally profound.

My mother and father placed him in a retirement home called Heart of the Valley, which had once been a hospital. It was on Harrison Street, near Oregon State University, from which my grandfather had graduated in 1922, back when it was known as Oregon Agricultural College. And it was just down the street from the SAE fraternity, which he had pledged as a college student and had supported for more than half a century as treasurer and grounds-keeper.

At first, my mother visited him every day, then every other day, then whenever she could between an active life of work, family, and volunteering. Every January she bought him a new calendar and used her calligraphic skills to write the dates extra large so he could see them. She decorated his room with family photos, awards he had received from the SAE house, and crayon drawings that his great-grandchildren had done. At Christmas she sent out cards in his name and taped the ones he received to the wall. His roommates had little on their walls; my grandfather had a virtual family shrine.

My mother took video footage at the beach cabin and showed him how the waves still crashed gloriously to shore at the cabin dubbed "Schumacher's Ocean Crest." She put on birthday parties for him which drew three generations of family. And she listened to him tell his stories of the past.

Weeks became months. Months became years. My mother kept visiting, often on her way home from work as a secretary on the Oregon State University campus. In the summer, she often arrived on bike; in the winter, with that quintessential Oregon icon in hand: the umbrella. Other family members occasionally dropped in to see him; so did some SAEs, sometimes serenading him with fraternity songs. But we were like war generals whose infrequent visits to the troops heralded more attention than deserved. My mother, on the other hand, was the foot soldier who fought the battle week in and week out.

She updated my grandfather on current events, read him stories that my sister-the-novelist and I had written, told the nurses when the radio needed to be turned on so he could listen to Oregon State football and basketball games.

She occasionally helped him into his wheelchair and took him places: to Chintimini Park for a Father's Day picnic; to the SAE house, where he could see the apple trees along 30th Street that he had nurtured for decades; to his old neighborhood, where he remembered nearly every house on the block.

My mother made my grandfather feel important. In 1992, the seventieth anniversary of the Oregon State University Class of '22 was held. Ten people showed up. Among them were Linus Pauling, a two-time Nobel Peace Prize winner and world-renowned chemist, and my grandfather, who had spent most of his life selling insurance and serving as an assistant co-op manager. Later I joked about what a thrill it must have been for him to rub shoulders with such a great man; indeed, I said, Mr. Pauling must have gone back to Palo Alto, California, and bragged far and wide about being a classmate of the legendary Benjamin F. Schumacher.

The event infused my grandfather with energy for weeks but, fact was, he was lonely. And in great pain. Occasionally, he would ask where Grammy was, and Mom would explain that she had died back in '82, and that would leave him sad. Once, my mother found him holding hands with a little lady friend in a wheelchair. With his permission, my mom bought him a present to give to the woman for Christmas.

All around him, death hung like a specter. It shuffled down the hallways. It called on his roommates with regularity; they came and went like motel guests. But ironically, it wasn't the nursing-home death—or even the prospect of his own—that pained my grandfather the most. It was lamenting the loss of his wife. It was losing friends he had known for literally 75 years. It was hearing that one of his seven grandchildren, a cousin of mine, had committed suicide. It was my mother having to tell him of my father's death in 1996.

She had considered not telling him at all; by this point, he might not have noticed that my father never came to visit anymore. But she decided he needed to know, so she told him. His eyes grew watery. "But now you don't have anyone to go home to," he said to her. And together, a father and daughter who had both outlasted their spouses cried.

She had never experienced that kind of closeness with the man before, even as a child. Their household had been efficient, well-ordered, and disciplined, but not particularly warm. In fact, in the years since she began visiting him in the nursing home, she had seen their respective pain and perseverance bind them more tightly than ever. Sometimes she would tell him things she had never told him before—that he was a good father, for example. And sometimes when she was leaving he would say, "Oh, what a wonderful, wonderful daughter...."

She was with him when he died, which was the way she wanted it. She did not want him to be alone. The nursing home had called to say it was time and, 15 minutes after my mother arrived, he was gone, as if he had waited. He was 98. He had lived for eight years since coming to the nursing home.

A nurse was called to confirm his death. It was Halloween, and she entered the room dressed as a clown. Some people might have thought that sacrilegious, but my mother did not. At a circus, she later reminded me, when something bad has happened—say a trapeze artist is having trouble—they send in the clowns. And in that room, something bad *had* happened. But, my mother says, it was also something good. For her father's pain was over. And he had lived a good and honorable life.

She gently laid his hand down, took one final look, and left the room. Almost 50 years before, it was here that she had said hello to her first child. And now, it was here that she said good-bye to her father.

You don't take care of your father because you think you're going to get some sort of reward, my mother once told me; you do it because it's just the right thing to do. But in the years that she sat by the man's side, he subtly passed on to her a love in his weakness that he had been unable to pass on to her in his strength. It was only part of the legacy he would leave, but it was an important part. And as she walked out of the nursing home for the final time, she realized it was true: It is the giver who receives.

My Grandfather Myself

> As efficient as the inner workings of an individual tree may seem, trees are actually far from self-sufficient. Solitary trees are rarely found in nature.
>
> —*North American Trees*

One of my grandfather's wishes was that I preside over his memorial service. I did so. It was a little different from what I imagine most services for 98-year-old men are probably like.

A few dozen college students, representing his beloved SAE house, volunteered to sing some fraternity songs. We listened to snippets of a taped interview I had done with him more than a decade before he died. And we laughed, which is something I think you should do when remembering someone.

We laughed about how he would design intricate work plans for each day he and I kept the grounds at the SAE house, as if he were General Eisenhower himself.

We laughed about how he had an affinity for documents, and how on the Christmas Eve in 1974 that I announced my engagement, he was so moved that, for reasons I've never quite understood, felt led to read a good portion of his insurance policy to the entire family.

We laughed about how the man, when he wasn't working, could talk—and talk and talk and talk. When the two of us were working at the SAE house together, we would eat our lunches on the concrete steps out back. He would talk; I would listen. Getting in a word when Benjamin F. Schumacher was talking was like trying to sprint across a freeway; the moments of opportunity were few and far between.

"Now, Bob," he would say, then launch into a story about fresh produce or Oregon State football or something else, straying off course—then, about the time you had forgotten the original subject, returning. He would wave at someone driving by and, before you knew it, he was talking about how that man once sold him a house and about that house's lousy plumbing system and about a plumber he knew at Camp Pendleton during his army days and about how awful mess-hall food tasted and—say, would I like to try some of the fine plums Granny had picked just yesterday?

His sentences were like one of those Model-Ts in an old Laurel and Hardy movie: traveling down a country road, then suddenly veering across a field and into a farmyard, crashing through a barn, scattering the chickens, plowing through a haystack, ripping down the clothesline full of laundry, knocking over a fruit stand, and then nonchalantly rejoining the country road, as if never having left it.

He talked of riding the rails in Eastern Oregon, of "the place at 305 33rd Street" (he believed strongly that former houses should be identified with complete addresses, even on second and third references) and about how he once got lost working on a fire crew in the Siskiyou Mountains in southern Oregon. In a unique theological twist, what saved him, he was convinced, was "praying to God in German."

My grandfather was to stories what triathletes are to sports; his endurance was legendary. And just when you were wondering if this race would ever end, he would jolt you awake with a "Now, Bob..." and make the transition from, say, swimming to bicycling.

Finally, we laughed about how he loved to chronicle things. He was a list guy. He labeled every plant he grew. He charted his gas mileage with a spiral notebook that he kept in his glove compartment. He even kept track of all the charities to which he donated.

I found this out in 1984 when I decided that Schu wouldn't be around forever, so I should sit down with him and a tape recorder and ask him some questions. Given his propensity for run-on sentences, I later realized this was a little like offering to buy lunch for a food-crazed friend at an all-you-can-eat buffet.

At one point, I noticed a copy of *Decision* magazine on the coffee table and, knowing that it was Billy Graham's magazine, I asked Grandpa what he thought of the man.

"Well, I'll tell ya what, Bob, he's not a half-bad guy," which, for my grandfather, was a description of the highest praise. "In fact, I don't mind telling you I just sent the guy 25 bucks."

Suddenly, he pulled out a spiral notebook and started listing other organizations he had sent donations to recently: Easter Seals, Oregon State University, the Dakota Indians, March of Dimes and—"Why, look here, your mom dinged me 20 bucks for the League of Women Voters."

The list continued: "World Vision, First Methodist Church, World Wildlife, National Federation for the Blind, Disabled Vets." And I realized that this was a runaway truck, a brakeless semi barreling down a steep mountain pass.

I kid you not: When he was finished, my grandfather had read the names of 87 organizations (audiotape doesn't lie) in what I'm sure must be some sort of record for Most Charitable Organizations Listed in a Single Sentence.

But lo, I must add an eleventh-hour confession to this story—a confession that says something about legacies and, for better or worse, about me: I have kept track of virtually every golf shot I've taken since 1977; long before spreadsheets made that a relatively simple task, I charted everything from Greens in Regulation to how much I paid for the round (average cost of an 18-hole round in 1977: $4.58; in 1998: $32.44).

I'm a label addict—a nearly pack-a-day Post-It Note user, a guy who practically buys spiral notebooks in bulk.

Last year, just for fun, I saved all the credit-card come-ons I got in the mail: 148.

When I was a newspaper columnist, I charted not only the date and subject of every column I wrote, but where the idea came from (reader, myself, colleague, editor, other) and how much response I got. (In 1988, a column on Puli, the freeze-dried dog, triggered 18 calls, ranking it third for the year behind one on a homeless teenager and one on a trip I took to Haiti.)

I can tell you the 440-yard splits of every cross-country workout I ever ran in high school. I can show you the banana-chips box Sally and I took on our first sailing trip together in 1972. I have a list describing the 14 different footballs my sons played with from 1983 to 1987, including the Nerf ball their cousin Mary chewed both ends off.

Finally, I have designed an intricate map detailing how to put up my Christmas lights each year. I use multicolored pens. I use solid lines to indicate strings of lights, dashes to indicate extension cords, and triangles to indicate three-way plugs.

Am I pathetic or what? It is a fallacy to think we are our "own" person; we are blends of many. I consider such compulsions and don't know whether to laugh or cry, whether to do some mental strutting or to call a therapist.

As I consider who I've become in this life, such discoveries remind me of something I find both touching and terrifying: I am my grandfather's grandson.

Carrying On

> Essentially, the same growth process that enables the tree to increase the length and diameter of its woody parts also functions to heal its wounds. If the end of a branch is broken off, the branch does not necessarily cease to grow.
>
> —*1001 Questions Answered About Trees*

In northwest California and southwest Oregon, some of the largest, thickest trees in the world grow. Trees are the largest and oldest living things on earth, and in this region, the redwoods are bark-sided skyscrapers. Some weigh as much as 600 tons, roughly four times the weight of the blue whales that commute north and south in the nearby Pacific Ocean.

In the Siskiyou National Forest, near the coastal community of Brookings, Oregon, I have stood at the base of some of these monarchs, which tower to heights of nearly a football field. I have marveled at trunks that are a double-garage-door wide. I have tried to imagine all the history that's played out since these trees began as something the size of sunflower seeds, marveled at having touched the bark of a tree that has been growing since the Middle Ages, the days of Genghis Khan and Marco Polo.

I am awed by their size and strength and longevity. But for all the majesty of these redwoods, I'm even more awed by a couple of wispy maples that stand just beyond our back fence in Eugene. One is about 20 feet tall, the other perhaps 15, standing side by side, like mother and child. Neither is thicker than the handle of a baseball bat. The larger of the two might be four times the weight of a sockeye salmon, not a blue whale. The two have been growing not since the days of Marco Polo, but since roughly the days of the Windows 95 release.

I suppose one reason I'm impressed with these trees is the same reason I'm impressed with underdogs in sports: there's something heroic in overcoming the odds, whether you're a person, a team, or a tree.

I suppose another reason is that these trees are right here in front of me. Unlike the towering redwoods, I can see and appreciate how far they've come in such a short time. I know their pasts. I watch their progress. I see them grow.

I suppose a final reason why I'm awed by the maples is that they remind me of Leighanne and Levi.

❧ ❧ ❧

Leighanne Sager's mother gave birth to her at age 16. It wasn't a pretty childhood. Leighanne didn't meet her father until she was eight months old. In many ways, she was raised by her grandparents. She knew nothing of stability. Her father divorced her mother, got custody of her, and they moved to another state. He remarried, then got divorced again. Meanwhile, her mother struggled with alcoholism and failed relationships, dying at age 34. Leighanne's life was one of constant change, adversity and, for a while, failed relationships.

Then He came along. Or maybe He was there all along; she just didn't notice. "The Lord," she explains, looking back. "I was tired of my life-style. I was ready. I gave my life to Him."

She was 26. It was January 1987. Then Mark came along. Leighanne had been staying with a cousin whose child had Mark Sager as a Sunday school teacher. "I was drawn to his spirit," says Leighanne. "He had a zest for life."

Mark's past had been everything Leighanne's had not been: He had come from a stable family, had seldom moved, and had embraced the love and grace of God. His roots grew deep in the things that mattered; Leighanne was just trying to establish some.

They wed in September 1987, but their marriage was buffeted from the start. In one stretch, Leighanne had a miscarriage, she lost her job at the YMCA, and the lumber mill where Mark worked went on strike. But they dug deep into their faith to persevere.

When the sky cleared, a rainbow appeared in the form of a son, Levi, born in October 1989. He was named after one of Mark's great-grandfathers.

Time rolled on. So did the Sagers. They found a niche in a nondenominational church. They carved out a cozy, if modest, life with what he made as a salesman and she earned as a Toys R Us clerk. Looking back, Leighanne doesn't remember trips to the Caribbean or new cars in the driveway; she remembers how excited she was the time Mark surprised her with a new electric mixer.

She remembers how Mark tickled Levi and took him four-wheeling in the snow and almost became a kid all over again, thanks to his son. She remembers how thrilled Mark was to have a new job as head of a city maintenance crew and how he loved to tell people about the peace he had found in Christ.

And she remembers the day in August 1994 when he went to the doctor thinking he had the flu, which led to a devastating discovery: Mark had leukemia.

He fought through one Job-esque trial after another: from a 104.7-degree fever to the loss of control in his facial muscles. At one point, he could not generate the moisture needed to protect his eyes, and they had to be sewn shut because of a reaction to radiation.

Hopes buoyed when Mark's brother proved a perfect blood-type match for a bone-marrow transplant. But it was a no-guaranty procedure. Despite it all, Mark got up in front of the church one day and talked about what he had been through. "At one point I asked God, 'Why are You doing this to me?' He spoke to my heart and said, 'It doesn't matter. Just trust Me.'"

The transplant would be considered successful after five years. But Mark's lasted only one. Following the operation, his body rejected the marrow; the leukemia returned.

It wasn't a pretty death. He kissed Leighanne on the forehead—the way he had kissed her each morning before he went to work. And then, on January 18, 1996, he died. He was 38.

Leighanne went home and told Levi that his father had "gone home to be with Jesus." Levi, six at the time, pondered the meaning.

"Great, Mom," he said at first. Then, as the news sunk deeper, he began to cry. And cry. And cry.

Leighanne held him tight, mother and son suddenly alone in the world.

❧ ❧ ❧

My wife had found the two maples in a rocky, weed-choked area near a fence, right next to each other. One was about two feet tall, the other not much more than a foot. Frail. Not looking so much like little trees as big weeds. Sally considered the odds of them making it in this location, grabbed the shovel, and went to work, making sure she got as much of the root ball as possible to ease the trauma of the transfer.

"We can put them between the fence and the street," she said. "They'll grow better there."

I silently scoffed and not-so-silently pointed out that if some dog didn't trample them before they reached fence-high status, home-run baseballs from the BBA (Backyard Baseball Association) would. "They're just over the left-field wall," I said. "They'll get ripped."

She gave me one of those ye-of-little-faith looks and handed me the shovel. "Dig," she said, and pointed with her toe. "Here and here."

I dug. She planted and watered. The saplings grew. And grew. And grew.

We did not have to wait five years to see if the transplant was successful. It was. After nearly three years since being uprooted, the trees are not only surviving, but thriving. They are about ten times the size they were when moved. Real trees with real leaves.

Their trunks are straight and true. Their branches are smooth and strong. And on this late-October day, their leaves are an alluring shade of green and yellow with the faintest touch of red—a testament to the power of the soil, the sun, and Oregon's abundant rain. They are not straight-edged redwoods, tickling the clouds, but then, size has never been the truest test of strength and beauty.

Last Thanksgiving, a man got up in front of the church that Leighanne attends—a man new to the church. It was a special service in which people were invited to stand and give thanks for what had happened in their lives the past year. As the man stepped forward, few recognized him.

He was, he said, new to the faith. And he had come to that faith, in part, because of the inspiration of a former coworker of his: Mark Sager. Leighanne referred to the man in a letter she wrote for the church on the two-year anniversary of Mark's death.

> "I have been so blessed to hear about and see the individuals on whom Mark's life has had an impact," she wrote. "There have been so many. Mark's courage in his illness gave many the courage to take their faith in Christ to a more serious level."

She wrote of what her journey had been like since Mark's "home going," as she called it.

> Healing did not really come until the second year...and now this third year is beginning and it feels a lot like a resurrection, as I sense a new direction in life for my son and I. The bottom line is we must trust God with all we are and all we go through, for He is the only sure thing in this world of unsure things.
>
> Trusting Him means to keep loving Him even though there are no answers, and uncertainty becomes a way of life. Grief can be a process for a new life if you allow it. It's like old fallen timber that decays and yet it is full of nutrients in which all kinds of new plant life can begin. We have experienced the Lord's peace and His refreshing us, though the past two years have been very much a time of dormancy, awaiting new sprouts of life.
>
> All glory to God. With love and adoration,
>
> —*Leighanne and Levi Sager*

If the letter talked of the challenges of living again after the death of someone near, it didn't talk about what that life actually looked like. It didn't talk about Leighanne homeschooling Levi, who has Attention Deficit Hyperactivity Disorder and isn't yet ready for the mainstream. About how she got involved with the church's missions board and began attending "The Grace Institute," an intense weekly exploration of the Scriptures. About attending two of Josh McDowell's Right from Wrong conferences on children in our changing culture. About Leighanne realizing her responsibility to not only help pass on Mark's legacy to Levi, but to pass on her own as well, realizing Mark would always be a part of her, but never would—nor should—be *all* of her.

The letter spoke of Mark's courage, but it didn't speak of her own. It didn't speak about how lots of people, especially those whose childhoods weren't pretty, fall back on some destructive habits when the storms of life blow strong, but Leighanne had not. Or how she's been reaching out to a longtime friend who had just attempted suicide for the fourth time. Or how she took Levi to the Oregon Dunes and marveled at his creativity and love of life, watching him race down the mountains of sand with his arms spread wide, pretending he was a sea gull.

"I envy that," she said later. "Growing up happy. It's peaceful to watch Levi grow up. He enjoys the moment."

The pain of losing Mark persists; at times, she says, it feels as if she has lost a limb. One morning, she awoke and felt a kiss on the forehead, only to realize Mark wasn't there. But she carries on.

She and Levi dropped by our house the other night. Leighanne is five feet tall and can't weigh more than 100 pounds; Levi, now nine, is small enough to pass for seven. They stepped out of—well, *dropped* out of—one of those mammoth pickups that you see driving up mountains of cinder blocks in the TV commercials.

"I'm a little sore," said Leighanne. "Just got back from a ten-mile bike ride with nine Cub Scouts."

As dusk descended on this October eve, Leighanne sat in our kitchen nook and shared about life before and after Mark Sager. Out in the living room, Levi, wearing one of my son's old football helmets, watched cartoons with Sally, and enlightened her about the world of Legos. And outside I could see the leaves of the two maples flutter blithely in the breeze, as if holding little fear of winter.

Treasures in Heaven

> If a healthy soil is full of death, it is also full of life....given only the health of the soil, nothing that dies is dead for very long.
>
> —*The Unsettling of America*

When our pastor spoke from the Book of Matthew about "not storing up for yourselves treasures on Earth, where moth and rust destroy," I thought about an auction I had once attended for a newspaper column I was writing.

It was no ordinary auction. The public could bid on unclaimed items that people had left behind in safe-deposit boxes. These items were once deemed so important that people paid money to have them safeguarded in steel.

War medals, diplomas, children's report cards...

I remember how we shuffled along, past the coin collections and pocket watches and jewelry, past small items sealed in plastic bags.

Rosaries, letters, train tickets...

It was all unclaimed property, the forgotten or overlooked possessions of owners now dead.

Boy Scout patches, a receipt from the Kuhio Hotel in Waikiki, and a child's color-crayon drawing of a bunny rabbit...

This is the stuff that people once deemed too valuable to keep at home, where it might be stolen, burned, or misplaced. Now it sat on a table, sealed in plastic, waiting for the highest bidder. Each bag was a mystery, the clues doing more to arouse curiosity than to provide answers. I read the immigration papers of Udolf Matschiner, who arrived at Ellis Island in 1906. Did he find what he was looking for in America?

Two marbles, three stones, and a belt buckle...

Why these things? Did they represent some special memory, some special person?

Passports, telegrams, newspaper clippings...

A yellowed article from a 1959 Los Angeles newspaper was headlined "Vlahovich's Mother Sobs at Guilty Verdict." A mother's son had been convicted of murder. The mother wept, pleading with the judge to spare her son. "Take my blood," she screamed. "Kill *me*." What happened? Did she watch her son die in San Quentin's electric chair?

Undeveloped film, birth certificates, marriage certificates...

The official business of life intermingled with the unofficial business of life: a lock of blond hair, a child's math paper, and a poem called "Grandmother's Attic," typed on a typewriter with a fuzzy *e*.

While up in Grandmother's attic today
In an old red trunk neatly folded away
Was a billowy dress of soft old grey
Of rose brocade were the panniers wide

With quilted patterns down the side
And way in the back against the wall
Of the little old trunk was an old silk shawl
Silver slippers, a fan from France
An invitation to a dance
Written across the program blue
Was "Agatha dear, may I dance with you?"

It was as if those of us at the auction had been allowed into hundreds of grandmothers' attics, the attics of unknown people.

Diaries, photographs, a newborn's footprint in ink...

"Store up for yourself treasures in heaven," said the pastor on that Sunday morning, "where moth and rust do not destroy, and where thieves do not break in and steal. For where your treasure is, there your heart will be also."

A Tree Planted by Water

In an hour on a summer day, a tall maple transpires about as much water as a hot tub holds. That's a lot of water to spread around in an hour, but not a drop is ever seen by someone lazing under the tree's branches as the water travels from earth through plant to air. Like the water in the maple, all the garden's water is on the move, and most of it is hidden from us.

—*Our Gardens Ourselves*

Trees stay alive with hidden reservoirs of water. Imagine, if you will, how a 200-foot redwood gets nourishment to its upper branches. The process does not begin with raindrops landing on some top-level needles. It begins when water that has soaked into the ground is taken in by the roots and propelled upward, in an apparent defiance of gravity. When droughts come, the healthier trees—the trees with a vast reservoir of nourishment—are the trees that will survive.

"Two weeks after Paul's death," says my sister-in-law Linda, "someone told us that 90 percent of marriages that go through the death of a child end in divorce. We were honest and admitted that we could see how that could happen."

Why didn't it? Because, she says, when her 16-year-old son died on the last day of 1994, swept away in an icy river, she had a hidden reservoir of hope. "The Holy Spirit was able to take all my truth legacies that I had stored throughout my life and bring them to my mind for my comfort and strength."

In speaking to a women's group three years after Paul's death, she talked of two kinds of legacies that sustained her: God's truth and people's modeling. She went back through her life and identified the pieces different people had put in her legacy puzzle: among them, a mother and father who taught her that pain was an integral part of life and you cannot run from it, and grandparents who modeled a similar steadfastness, and always looked for the best in people.

Then she talked about God's truth—the promises that she had absorbed since learning what she calls "truth legacy one": "Jesus loves me, this I know, for the Bible tells me so."

Just as it takes time for a tree to build a system of nourishment, so does it take time for people to develop such a system. Some of her "truth legacies" came from experiences—the time when the family had three children younger than four and her husband, Greg, was working nights and going to seminary during the day. Others came from books. All were necessary to their surviving this tragedy.

In the aftermath of Paul's death, Linda remembers herself and Greg realizing they had to make a choice: to run away from God and into, as Linda calls it, "some mythical light," or "to walk into the darkness with Him." She remembers realizing that they could not be led by their feelings—because both she and Greg were empty and angry and bitter—but by their faith.

"While it is well with our souls," she said, "our hearts are still broken."

Other circumstances compounded the second year after Paul's death. Their daughter, Traci, got married and left home. Their other child, Brad, left for college in California. And it would have been Paul's senior year of high school, which brought forth an abundance of "he-would-have-been" reflections.

Friction increased. The marriage teetered on the brink of failure. Linda recalled the legacy of her grandparents: *Always look for the best in people.* She looked for the best in Greg.

"We weren't supposed to be in the empty-nest place of our lives yet, but we were," said Linda. "We both had to learn to communicate with each other around life without kids. Not an easy task; old patterns die hard. There were days when I felt we might not make it to our twenty-fifth anniversary."

But the key word, she said, was *felt*. "I knew I could not let those feelings dictate how life would play itself out. I had a choice to make. There were days that I did not *want* to do the right thing or say the right thing, but I did. It was very much a deliberate action. It was definitely a battle."

A teacher, she would drive to work each morning listening to songs that spoke of God's faithfulness. At first, she would sing out loud, but when the tears came, she sang only in her heart.

"What legacies have been left to you?" she asked her audience. "Look for them. Rely on them. Let them be your link to strength."

She paused.

"What legacies are you leaving? You are leaving one whether you are planning to or not. Make choices each day that will leave a legacy for others to follow in their walk with God."

She then referred to Jeremiah 17:7,8, about trees planted by water, about roots by the stream, about leaves that are always green despite the drought.

It is the hidden process of hope, and it begins deep within and long ago.

Scattering Seeds Anew

Second Wind

What do we plant when we plant the tree?
We plant the ship, which will cross the sea.
We plant the mast to carry the sails;
We plant the plant to withstand the gales.
The keel, the keelson, and beam and knee;
We plant the ship when we plant the tree.

—Anonymous

Fern Ridge Lake lies calm on this April morning. It's just the three of us at Richardson Point: Me. My mother. And *At Last*, the dream sailboat she and my father had ultimately found after starting out with an eight-foot pram and a bed-sheet sail.

A sailboat, like life itself, looks simple from the outside but is amazingly complex. A sailboat is wire and rope and Dacron and fasteners, all of which seem to be called something else, like stays and sheets and jibs and turnbuckles.

My father, the man who had known every piece on this boat and fabricated a few himself, died last year. In a sense, he had taken the secret code with him: how to rig a 22-foot, 2300-pound Catalina; raise a 25-foot mast; and get it all in the water, right-side up.

For as long as I can remember, my father spearheaded this spring ritual in our family, whether the vessel was a 12-foot fishing boat or the considerably more complicated *At*

Last. It was never a smooth experience with my father; in fact, on opening day the spring before he died, we cast off and watched our rudder slowly disintegrate in our wake, which makes it rather difficult to steer. But he was one of those guys with the gift of improvisation, and would always find a way to fix something.

Now he is gone and it is time for Mom and me to go it alone. Time to venture into uncharted water. Time, in keeping with the season of springtime, Passover, and Easter, to start anew.

I look at scrawled notes from last year's setup—"pull down boom vang and tie off"—and his crude sketches that look as if from a Pictionary game. *Hmmm.* My mother stands in the boat, which is propped on its trailer like a pre-op patient on a gurney.

"Where does this line go?" she asks. I look at the line. I look at the boat. I look at my deepest sense of pride, and wonder if I should assure this 71-year-old woman that I'm in complete control.

"I have no idea," I say.

Therein lies the challenge of starting over: not having all the answers, but being willing to keep rigging the boat anyway. It has something to do with faith in that which cannot be seen, and imagining results even if we can't visualize the process that will help create those results.

A week ago, a friend of mine gave up a week's vacation and flew south to help his drug-addicted brother start his life over. Meanwhile, back at the launch, Mom and I begin untangling a less-significant mess—a ball of wires and ropes and bungee cords that look like the contents of a garage-sale grab box.

"It's like putting together a giant puzzle," says my mother. As the morning warms, we realize a few of the pieces are missing. Gone is a custom metal fitting needed to secure the radio antenna atop the mast. A trip home to retrieve it would cost us at least two hours.

I look at Mom. She looks at me. In an instant, we both know the answer as sure as we know from whence it came: duct tape—my father's unconventional, all-purpose fixer.

In the 42 years the two of us were alive together, the man taught me more than how to fix things with duct tape. He taught me right from wrong, respect for people and nature, the art of independence. I wish he had taught me more, wish he could have been more this and less that. But in forging on, we must reach back and take the good things we've been left, and leave the rest. Duct tape may not be the perfect solution, but for now it will work. The alternative is to stay dockside, moored to regret.

A few days before this launch, I finished a courageous book by Patricia Raybon, a University of Colorado professor, that speaks of the same stuff. Called *My First White Friend,* it tells of the African-American writer's journey to overcome the hatred she felt for white people because of the discrimination she has faced.

Embroiled in bitterness, she finally reached for what worked, something a bit unconventional in our power-hungry culture: forgiveness. Inspired in part by the example set by Jesus, she forgave people for the hurt they had inflicted on her.

"It was," she writes, "like a veil lifting, like scales falling from hardened, hopeless eyes."

In forging on, we must have the strength to forgive, the will to humble ourselves, the courage to start anew.

Mom and I connect the forestay (the wire thingamajig on the front of the tall, skinny deal) to the trailer's winch. I stand atop the cabin and step the mast. Mom cranks on the winch. Slowly, the metal tube rises in the sky.

"You sure you can handle that?" I ask.

It is a stupid question, really, from a son who has seen his mother handle plenty in the last year and a half. The death of her husband. The death of her father. And a refusal to sit in the doldrums, surrendering to loss. In the back of her car, she has a pair of swim fins; in a few months, she will leave for an exploration of the Galapagos Islands.

Looking at a sketch left by my father, we're able to connect two deep-cycle batteries and ten loose wires, and power up. We get the motor running. We feed the mainsail onto the boom, thread the jib onto the forestay.

I think of a friend of mine who has sailed through storms I've never faced. He fought in Vietnam. Lost one of his closest friends to a booby trap. Got word a few months later that his father in Oregon had been killed in a log-truck accident. Battled the demons of drugs. After straightening out his life, lost his first wife in what was supposed to be routine surgery.

Hardship at hurricane force. But on this day, as my mother and I prepare to launch a boat, he's preparing to launch a church. On Easter Sunday, my friend Larry, with new hope and a new wife who supports his dream, will unfurl ValleyHills Community Church.

In forging on, we must wait patiently on God to provide that second wind, even if that wind might blow from a direction we might not choose. Sailboats, James Michener once wrote, do poorly when the wind is directly behind them. "What is needed," he wrote, "is a wind slightly opposed to the ship, for then tension can be maintained and juices can flow and ideas can germinate, for ships, like men, respond to challenge."

By noon, *At Last* slides off her trailer and into the lake. She is back where she belongs, looking elegant, even with a dash of duct tape atop her mast.

In the middle of Fern Ridge Lake, four hours and a few bloody fingers after we started this process, Mom and I chow down on ham sandwiches. She offers me a high-five hand slap. And then it is time.

"Ready?" she says.

"Ready."

We hoist the sails, and a new season begins.

Shooting Stars

> There is a melancholy, almost unnatural stillness to a deciduous forest in winter. The tree trunks rise blank and gaunt from the snow like soiled bones. But as lifeless and forbidding as it may seem, the winter landscape is in fact a vital starting point for the dynamic workings of the forest's perennial cycle.
>
> —*Forests*

He would have been 20 today. I know that because on the same October day in 1978 that we learned that my nephew Paul had been born, we learned that my wife was pregnant with our first son. And Ryan was born about eight months after Paul. It is a date etched deep in my memory.

He would have been pleased to know that, as of today, Penn State is 5-1 and ranked tenth in the country. Paul was born in Oregon and lived in Wyoming and Washington, but when it came to college football, he loved a team from the east: Penn State. It was a quirky choice that was quintessential Paul, a kid who was refreshingly himself; popular, yes, but not one who felt he had to validate his worth by following the crowd.

A few years ago, on a dry, nearly windless summer day, a young maple tree in our front yard—about five inches thick and 25 feet tall—simply snapped at ground level and fell over. It made no sense. No sign of disease. No advance warning. Then, in an instant: gone.

That's the way it was with Paul. He was just 16. He and his older brother were on Washington's Olympic Peninsula, hiking in a canyon through which an icy river rumbled. It was December 31, 1994. He slipped and fell down a 40-foot embankment into the river. In an instant: gone. They found his body in June. As I said, it made no sense.

A couple of nights ago, I got an e-mail from Paul's father, Greg. My brother-in-law is a pastor in Shelton, and we correspond regularly, often dropping our guards to get beyond the "everything's-fine" analyses of life.

"We're a little low, thinking about the events of 20 years ago, but that should be expected I guess," he wrote, then referred to a recent trip on which our families had gotten together. "Seeing Ryan actually helps more than it hurts. It gives us perspective and a sense of what Paul would be like. That is good. It will be good to have a measuring stick over the years, but of course it is not the same."

I e-mailed back: "Yes, he would have been 20. But he WAS 1, 2, 3, 4, 5, 6, 7, 8, 9, 10, 11, 12, 13, 14, 15 and 16, and he was a blessing to us all for those years. We won't forget him. Or you."

Replied Greg: "Thanks for the note. It is hard to think about what we had because what we lost keeps getting in the way. Yours was a reminder that we should try to move in that direction."

Much of this book speaks of older generations passing on legacies to younger generations; of grandparents leaving behind values and expectations for their children and grandchildren; of heritages rooted deep in the soil of time. But legacies are not age-dependent. True, they can be strengthened by time in much the same way a tree can be strengthened by time. But the value of a legacy is more closely tied to the character of the legacy-giver than the life span of the legacy-giver.

While backpacking high in Washington's North Cascades, I once saw a falling star above a place called Monogram Lake. That star flamed through the sky for only a split second, yet I still remember it more than a decade later. Why? Because its legacy was dependent not on its longevity, but on its brilliance. Its rarity. In fact, its briefness *enhanced* its legacy because, at least in my eyes, it accomplished so much with so little time.

On the other hand, I've written a story about a 75-year-old woman who spent most of her life fighting city hall to allow her to keep as much garbage on her property as possible. What did longevity do for her legacy, other than compound the garbage left behind? I've written about other people who have lived a long time, one of whom drank himself to death, and another who died a bitter man because nobody could ever live up to his expectations. Again, their life spans neither enhanced nor ruined their legacies, because legacies are character-dependent, not time-dependent.

Like that shooting star, my nephew was both brilliant and rare. Not necessarily brilliant in the way we usually use the word (i.e., a mental genius, though he was smart), but brilliant in another sense of the word: "distinctive," says Webster's.

Paul was not chained to here-today-gone-tomorrow fashion trends. He didn't crave the spotlight. He was a blend of 16-year-old mischievousness and a more mature understanding of what mattered in life.

In his time on earth, he endeared himself to people around him. He invested in relationships. He invested in God. He loved his parents and brother and sister. He never grumbled when I asked him to play a shepherd in the family's annual way-off-Broadway Christmas play.

He was courageous in his dealing with diabetes, and helped a friend learn to deal with it herself. He outdueled one of my sons in a "burp-off." He set a mean pick in driveway basketball. And he loved the simple things in life, like the time we filled up an old waterbed, placed it in our backyard, and watched Paul, his brother, and my two sons wrestle, roll, flip, and flop on the thing for hours.

Clearly, he touched people's lives. In the small town beside Puget Sound where he lived, more than 500 people crowded the church for his memorial service. A friend wrote a story in the local paper and said the high school would never be the same without him. Family members whom I had never seen cry, cried. His brother, Brad, wrote him a letter that said, "God gave you to me as a little brother for 16 years and I will always cherish those 16 years. You were the best brother, the best friend and the best companion. It looks like it's your turn to look after me; I tried my best to take care of you."

A year after his death, nearly 100 people gathered at the bridge high above the river in which he died, to remember him. To grieve once again. To acknowledge that he had not been forgotten, and to vow that he wouldn't be.

Some people's legacies blow away in the wind soon after the casket is lowered or the ashes scattered. But the more impact someone has had on people while living, the more impact he or she will have on people when gone. Which prompted me recently to ponder Paul's legacy.

How is the world any different because this young man lived for 16 years, two months, and seven days? How are people any different because he lived and died? How am *I* any different because he lived and died?

Legacies are like a half-moon hanging in the night sky: We see only part of the whole that we know is there. Whether we see it or not, the moon has a huge impact on the seas that cover most of the planet Earth; its position and gravitational pull, in essence, create two high tides and two low tides around the globe each day. The moon, then, has a visual impact on thousands of miles of coastlines. The moon determines when a ship can leave a harbor, where a town has been built, and, of course, when the crabbing is good. Even though we cannot see the process in action, we can see the results.

With Paul, I can only describe that part of the moon that I can see, and I realize it is but a sliver. But I can say that because Paul Scandrett lived and died, his father and I are far closer than we would have been otherwise. Our relationship has always been cordial and smooth. But for some reason, Paul's death infused each of us with new freedom to be more bluntly honest about our lives with each other. In late-night e-mails, Greg has felt free to share his pain. That has made me feel free to share some of my struggles. And we've been able to encourage and challenge each other like never before.

I can say that because Paul lived and died, I got to touch the lives of nearly 100 men who attend the church Greg pastors—and had the privilege of having my life touched by theirs. In part because he had grown to know me better following Paul's death, Greg asked me to lead a weekend men's retreat. It came at a point in my life in which my faith was at slack tide. My fathering commitment had gotten backburnered by my being too busy. My wife was away in the Dominican Republic. And I was wrestling with the decision of our pastor—a close friend, mentor, and model—to leave our church and move 2000 miles away. But that weekend with Greg's church helped rejuvenate my life and my faith.

I can say that because Paul lived and died, I'm less apt to take my own sons for granted. Whenever I hear a siren when I'm home and the boys are not, I immediately think of Paul. And I'm reminded of how easily even the closest people in our lives can be taken for granted.

I can say that because Paul lived and died, his extended family—particularly the men—are far less reluctant to hug one another. That we have a new appreciation for what good-bye might mean. That we sense a closeness that sometimes only adversity can bring.

I can say that because Paul lived and died, hundreds of people in Greg's church witnessed the Light of the world in the darkest time of a couple's life. Listening to your pastor preach on trusting God during painful times is one thing; watching your pastor and his wife actually *do* that trusting is quite another.

And I can say that because Paul lived and died, hundreds of thousands of *Focus on the Family* readers had the opportunity to be inspired by the promises of God and the courage of Greg and his wife, Linda, following an article I wrote for the magazine after Paul died.

Again, this is just the sliver of moon I can see. The legacy Paul left for others will be different from the legacy he left for me. And who knows about the ways in which Paul's legacy might have been transferred from one person to another? How many people in that Shelton church recommitted themselves to trusting God more because of Greg and Linda's example? And as these people trusted more, and their lives bore the fruit of the Spirit, how many others were inspired by those examples, and perhaps took a step of faith themselves?

After reading of Greg and Linda's pain of losing a son, how many *Focus on the Family* readers might have become more like the father of the prodigal son and welcomed home a wayward child? And how many of those wayward children might have softened their hearts and made changes in their lives that will help them grow up to be the parents God would have them be, to pass on those values of love and forgiveness to their own children?

Planting a tree is an act of faith. There are no guarantees that the seed will ever take root, or that if it does, it will become a seedling, or that if it becomes a seedling, it will become a sapling. There are no guarantees that even if that sapling grows to maturity, it won't suddenly fall to earth on a windless day.

But we plant. We trust. We hope. We dream. And if our dreams crash down, we weep. We grieve. And keep on trusting.

In the aftermath of Paul's death, I was inspired by a poem by author, poet, and farmer Wendell Berry, part of which says:

> For we are fallen like the trees, our peace
> Broken, and so we must
> Love where we cannot trust.
> Trust where we cannot know,
> And must await the wayward-coming grace
> That joins living and dead…

I was also inspired by a sermon about trusting God even "when the lights go out." The pastor quoted author Annie Dillard, who writes, "You do not have to sit outside in the dark. If, however, you want to look at the stars, you will find that darkness is required."

"There are," explained the pastor, "some things about God that cannot be known simply when things are going well, when things are under control. And there are things about God you cannot understand when the lights are on. God only reveals certain things in the dark."

I might be tempted to pass off such wisdom as eloquent advice easily offered from a pastor not really knowing the pain of loss. But the sermon came less than two months after my nephew died. And it came from his father, a man who understands all about darkness—and the brilliance of shooting stars.

The Empty Chair

The best time to plant a tree was twenty years ago.
The second best time is now.

—*The Simple Act of Planting a Tree*

Dear Sir,

We have never met, but I know your son. He was the kid at the banquet the other night who won the Most Inspirational award. His coach, teammates, and parents clapped wildly for him. Heck, even the pizza guy gave him a thumbs up.

But where were you?

I know you're a busy man. You do important work. You make lots of money. And none of us can make every game or season-ending banquet. But you don't make any games or any banquets. You didn't make it the year he won the "most coachable" award either.

That night, while driving your son to the banquet, we asked if you and your wife might be coming later. "They said they might come," your son told us, "but watch. They won't."

Over the years, I've worked with hundreds of young people through coaching and helping groups of teenagers put out a weekly section at the newspaper where I work. I've gotten to know dozens of those young people fairly well. Your son is among the smartest, most responsible, most caring, and appealingly-off-the-wall young men I've ever met.

But you don't seem to notice that. Or his 3.9 GPA. Or the fact that he's working two jobs because he wants to go to college so badly and you apparently aren't willing to give him much financial aid. What you seem to notice is when he gets a "B." Or parks his car where you don't like it. Or leaves an occasional dish in the sink instead of putting it in the dishwasher.

How do I know this? Because he occasionally mentions you. Because his friends mention you. Because even if he won't admit it, he desperately wants your approval. And because you're way more important to him than you must think you are.

I've spent my entire career as a reporter and editor so I understand that every story has two sides. And I admit I haven't heard yours. Maybe your son is a Jekyll-and-Hyde type who acts differently around you than he does around others. Maybe I'm just another fan in the stands who, from a distance, doesn't understand what's really going on in this game. Maybe his friends who notice the same things he notices about you are too biased to recognize the truth.

But I think I'm a fairly good judge of character, and your son has it. I think you've got a great kid. He's not perfect. But he's got a great mind, great vision, a great heart.

The irony: Part of the reason your son is such a cool kid probably has something to do with you. Children don't grow up in vacuums; they're a complex compilation of genes, experiences, influences, environments, and God-given gifts. Parents have a more profound impact on who their children ultimately become than anyone else. To some degree, your son is a reflection of who you are.

That should make you proud. But does it? The fact is, if I told your son that, in some ways, he was a reflection of you, he would probably disagree. Because what scares him most about growing up is that he might become like you.

Still, I know you've had a positive influence on him. Maybe it was when he was younger, when life was simpler. Before the divorce and the remarriage. Before your son started feeling like he was a third wheel, an afterthought, the kid who parks his car in the wrong spot. A drain on your six-figure income. Someone who seemed to be more than enough for everybody else—teachers, coaches, friends, college recruiters—but could never be good enough for his father.

The other day, I heard an expert on adolescents say that our kids need five positive affirmations from us for every criticism in order to grow up with a healthy respect for who they are. How's your batting average?

Mine, I know, is way lower than it should be. I think of how easily I get immersed in my own work, church, and play, and overlook my sons. I think of how easy it is to assume that they know how proud I am of them, how easy it is to rationalize not taking three minutes and jotting them a note of encouragement.

When was the last time you affirmed your son? I get the idea that the two of you don't spend a whole lot of time communicating, period, so you might not know all the things your son does right.

Did you know that when one of his friends at work was struck with leukemia, your son was among the few who had the courage, and compassion, to visit him? That he says "please" and "thank you"? That the kids on the youth basketball team he coached think he's the coolest cat since Michael Jordan?

Forgive me if I'm overstepping my bounds here. Maybe I should realize that he's your son, not mine, and that this is none of my business. Maybe I should just chuck this letter and realize that the cement is dry on this relationship and it's not going to change. Maybe I shouldn't care.

But it's so hard to see two people who desperately need one another and yet who are so utterly disconnected. It's a shame. It's a waste. Because it doesn't *have* to be this way.

I keep wondering why you're so critical of your son. I can't help but think you're bitter about something deep inside you, and your son pays the price for that bitterness. Perhaps you thought if you got a good education and a high-paying job that life would be fulfilling, and it's not. Perhaps you were raised in a home where legalism, not love, ruled the day. Perhaps you were raised by a toe-the-mark father for whom nothing was good enough, a father who was bitter at life and made you pay the price for that bitterness.

If that was the case, I'm sorry. But if it was, don't you see what you're doing? You're perpetuating the legacy you inherited. You're keeping alive the very stuff that you probably railed against when you were your son's age. You're, in essence, condoning—not condemning—the values that somehow snuffed out your zest for life.

I hurt for you. And I want to help if I can.

You seem to be living your life for the meaningless minutia of now—who will care in ten years where your kid parked his car?—and investing little for the future.

I have a good friend, my brother-in-law, who would give anything to have his son park in the wrong place or leave dishes in the sink. But his son isn't around. He slipped and fell into a river; they found his body six months later.

It tears me apart that my brother-in-law, nearly four years after losing his 16-year-old son, still misses his kid so much that I can almost feel the ache from 300 miles away. And, according to your son, you often act like he is just an inconvenience.

In a few months, your son will leave for college. And you may never again have a chance to connect with him. I read his college essay recently—he needed some copyediting help—and the theme of it was how he wanted to go conquer the world. How he wanted to prove to the world that he could make it—without you.

In a letter, I told him that was the wrong reason for wanting to soar—so he could look down at you and remind you that he didn't need you after all. Because I think he does need you; but to admit it means having to stand on one side of a deep canyon and look at all the nothingness between the two of you. And that emptiness hurts too much. So it's easier to just pretend there's nobody on the other side.

I told him that even if you seldom showed it, you probably loved him. And that if what empowered him to "succeed" was to spite you, he, too, would be perpetuating this legacy of bitterness.

In my 19 years of fathering, the most challenging part has been admitting my faults, saying I'm sorry, and being willing to change. Slowly, I'm learning. Yesterday, I heard a sermon at church from a man whose son was aching so badly for the approval of his demanding father that he was ready to commit suicide. But the story had a happy ending. Why? Because the father, in brokenness, was courageous enough to admit his failures. He was so committed to righting a wrong that he humbled himself and just said: *God, I can't do it alone. I need You. Help me become what I need to become for my kid.*

The man then read us a letter from his son that he got recently, years since their falling out. In it, his son said how proud he was to have the man as his father. Imagine that. Seriously: What it would feel like to read a letter from your son that said how proud he was to have you as a father?

It could happen. You have the power to help make it happen. In the time it would take to say "I'm sorry," you could infuse your son with a hope that he's waited nearly a lifetime to have. If you could back up those two words with a true commitment to change, you could create something that will last a lot longer than that shiny new car in the garage, or that recent trip to Hawaii. And if you could somehow hug that young man with the same fervor with which you probably hugged him when he was small, you could melt an iceberg of anger that's been growing inside of him for years.

Scary isn't it? But every noble act is a difficult act; risk without danger is no risk at all. Sure, it's a two-way street; like us all, your son isn't perfect and needs to be willing to make some changes, too. And, of course, there are no guarantees here. Your son might not take the olive branch you offer him; he might be too intent on looking for hidden agendas to appreciate your humility. You can't undo the past in an instant. But you can begin.

It's frightening, the thought of change. But if you don't take such a risk—and as adults, we're the ones who need to lead these reconciliatory attempts—you're *guaranteed* of one thing: You and your son will spend the rest of your lives standing on either side of that canyon, staring at these little specks on either side. Years may pass. Decades may even pass. Then, one day, one speck will suddenly be gone and the man that remains will be faced with one question: Was it worth it?

Was it worth never trying to bridge that gap? Was the price you paid worth what you got in return?

A few years ago, over pitchers of pop and slices of pizza, your son was honored as the most inspirational kid on his team. But I believe he would have traded the plaque and all the clapping and hollering for just one simple nod of approval from the father who wasn't there.

There's still an empty chair next to him at that table.

Pepperoni OK?

The Baton

> Every tree, like every man, must decide for itself—will it live in the alluring forest and struggle to the top where alone is sunlight, or give up the fight and content itself with the shade.
>
> —*Ernest Thompson Seton*

East of Bend, in Oregon's high desert country, I await the start of the five-mile road race. It is Labor Day 1998. In the distance, the Cascade Mountains look like weathered chalets in need of fresh trim, having not seen snow since June. St. Charles Hospital, where my two sons were born, juts up amid the junipers and sagebrush. Next to me, runners stretch and talk in the gathering heat.

It has been 15 years since I called this place home, and I've returned not so much for me, but for him. For the guy who was something of a mentor to me when I was a young father, though he probably never even knew it. For the guy who reminded me of Eric Liddel, the *Chariots of Fire* Scotsman who loved to run, but loved God even more. For the guy they named the race after.

The starting gun shatters the morning quiet. We're off. Hundreds of runners—men and women, boys and girls—all wearing race numbers emblazoned with the same thing: Eagles-Chuck Austin Memorial Run.

❧ ❧ ❧

He was, some people will tell you, larger than life. His brother said as much, right after telling the story about how when the two were little boys, Chuck would lie in bed without a shirt on, eating celery and carrots, his belly button filled with salt.

I met him when I was 22 and fresh from the University of Oregon (his alma mater, too). He was 40 at the time. I attended the same church he did.

A local businessman, Chuck would occasionally drop something off at the newspaper where I was the sports editor; when he came in, it was like a cool breeze through cottonwoods.

I worked in an environment of deadlines, pressure, swearing, and smoke—not the kind of place conducive to growing the scriptural "fruit of the Spirit," particularly forgiveness.

My editor, who had all the warmth of Old Man Potter, was forever growling about my spelling and grammar, which I admit, wasn't stellar. Once he called to say I had misspelled another word. Usually he was right, but this time I didn't think so. I checked a dictionary, confirmed I was right, and marched—OK, *nervously walked*—into the man's office, dictionary in hand.

The man looked in the dictionary for quite some time, then looked up at me. "Welch," he said, as I eagerly awaited the apology, "get a new dictionary."

In a work world peppered with such interactions, I learned to appreciate the gentleness of Chuck Austin. Though deeply devoted to God, he related well to all sorts of people, even those who scorned his faith. When speaking to our young-marrieds class at church, he inspired us, without raising his voice, to dig deeper for God. When complimented, he never swelled with pride. When confronted, he never battled back in bitterness.

Once, at an Oregon alumni luncheon, I heard a former college football teammate of his chide him about his faith. "I hear you went and got religion," the man said. "So, what are you going to do, become a priest?"

Chuck laughed lightly and said, "Well, I guess I've learned you don't need to wear your collar backwards to minister for God."

Other than in church or at the newspaper, I mainly saw Chuck Austin on the streets and roads. He was a runner—not particularly fast, but through relentless training, extremely durable. He was the first University of Oregon graduate to complete the venerable Boston Marathon, and had the plaque to prove it. His time was 2 hours and 58:55 minutes.

Chuck Austin was handsome. Tan, with rugged skin. Slightly oversized ears that gave him an almost boyish look. George Clooney eyes. A smile that could melt Deschutes River ice in the coldest January.

He was smart. His pastor-father and Dallas Theological Seminary had molded him into something of a scriptural scholar. His prowess in the real-estate business was well-known. He was deeply involved in Bend, the small central Oregon town where he had lived since he was 12. Church. Young Life. United Way. School board chairman. He even ran for the state legislature.

He had the kind of family you would see in a photo studio's display window: a lovely wife and five children, white-teethed and innocent, the likeness of their father unmistakable. They skied together, ran together, played soccer together.

They lived in a two-story white house a stone's throw from Mirror Pond, a sort of "Leave-It-to-Beaver" dwelling dwarfed by pines and splashed with the red, white, and blue of an American flag—right across the street from my boss, the guy who thought I needed a new dictionary.

When you're a young father and see a man like Chuck Austin, you think to yourself: Someday, I want to be like that man. But you never stop to think that such a man would ever leave this setting, would ever hurt, would ever wind up living in a condominium far away. You never stop to think that life changes, that strong bodies fail, that eagles fall from the sky.

❧ ❧ ❧

The trouble began in the early eighties. Oregon's recession had buffeted Chuck's real-estate holdings, and someone double-crossed him to seal his financial fate; his family was forced to move. He, his wife, Bea, and the two teenage children who hadn't already left home, left Bend in 1982. Chuck found a job with the federal government, and the family relocated to Bellevue, Washington, just east of Seattle.

A year later, we moved, too—ironically, also to Bellevue, where I went to work for the *Journal-American* newspaper. We wound up going to the same church as Chuck and Bea did—the four of us trying to find contentment in what seemed like a foreign land.

We grew to know each other better. After living all our lives within a quick drive of relatives, my wife, Sally, and I were on our own, trying to raise four- and one-year-old sons. On our first Easter away from home, Chuck and Bea had us over for dinner. In the years to come, their teenage son and daughter occasionally baby-sat our boys. We got together from time to time, linked by our faith and our Oregon roots. Once, while Chuck and I walked my boys to a playground, I felt compelled to ask him for advice on fathering.

"Tell me something that will help me when my kids get to be the age of yours," I asked, though I never really expected my children to actually *be* that old.

What he told me surprised me. I expected some deep theological treatise on parenting. Instead, he said this: When forbidding your kids from doing something with other kids that you deem unwise, try to find something fun—yet safe—to replace that something with. "Kids," he said, "need to have fun. And if you're creative in coming up with a replacement, they'll realize you care about them, and aren't trying to stifle them."

In a few years, we left for another church. Then, almost seven years after arriving, we left Bellevue to return to our roots in Oregon's Willamette Valley. In September 1989, only a few miles from where we had moved to, a college student got a phone call. It was Steve Austin, Chuck's oldest son, then 25 and a student at the University of Oregon. The phone call brought news about his father.

He had pancreatic cancer.

The time had come. Nine months later, on a Sunday morning in June 1990, the family gathered in Chuck and Bea's living room in Bellevue for the ceremony. On the scratchy tape recording, you hear the occasional cry of a baby—Chuck's granddaughter Conley—occasional laughter, and some quiet sobbing.

You hear the family joining together to sing "O Worship the King," Chuck's then-82-year-old father leading a prayer and reading some Scripture, including Hebrews 12:1,2:

> Therefore, since we are surrounded by such a great cloud of witnesses, let us throw off everything that hinders and the sin that so easily entangles,

> and let us run with perseverance the race marked out for us. Let us fix our eyes on Jesus, the author and perfecter of our faith, who for the joy set before him endured the cross.

Finally, you hear the tired voice of Chuck Austin, a man whose race was nearly over. "Hebrews 12," he says, "is the succession of the 'heroes of faith' in Chapter 11....The picture I see is like the mass of people at the Boston Marathon, lining the streets for mile after mile, cheering us on....All these heroes—those who have gone on before us—standing on the sidelines, cheering us on, saying: 'You can do it in the power of the Lord Jesus.'

"It's not an 880 or a mile or a 440 race, but a marathon—a marathon combined with a relay. Run with persistence, with endurance, with perseverance."

Weak and tired, he pauses. He illustrates the story with an anecdote involving Connie, his youngest daughter—how, when struggling to finish a race that he was also running, she fixed her eyes on the back of his shirt and vowed to not look away until she finished. She did.

He pauses again. "That's the goal I have for each one of you." He wasn't sure if his race was ending, he says, but if it was, he wanted his children to know that he would be there for them, cheering them on.

On the tape, you hear the rustling of something: gifts, it turns out. Something for his five children. Not store-bought gifts, but hand-crafted gifts that each of his children came forward to receive: wooden laminated batons, the kind a track athlete hands to a teammate in a relay race. On each one, Chuck had written a different child's name, with a simple exhortation: "Keep on running with your eyes fixed on Jesus! Love, Dad."

He died two days later. He was 54. At his memorial service, the opening song—played on the piano by his daughter

Lynette—was the theme song from his favorite movie, *Chariots of Fire*.

❧ ❧ ❧

The Eagles-Chuck Austin Memorial race is over. It doesn't matter where I finished or how fast I ran. Such numbers are meaningless. What matters is 300 people coming together to run and to remember. What matters is the pastor of the church that sponsors the race explaining to the crowd how the race is named not only for Chuck and for the road the church is on, but for Isaiah 40:31, which says "those who wait on the Lord shall renew their strength; they shall mount up with wings like *eagles*, they shall run and not be weary, they shall walk and not faint (NKJV)."

To the very end, Chuck Austin was never content with living in the shade; instead, he struggled to the top, where alone is the sunlight. His ascent was not like that of so many men, who trample others to earn their glory. He did not climb so he could beat his chest and say, "Look what I did." But to point to God and say, "Look what He did."

Chuck Austin was not perfect—even his children will tell you that—but his was a humble ascent that brings to mind the Oswald Chambers line about how "crises always reveal character."

His character shone through when he lost his fortune and, instead of blaming or getting bitter or suing the man who double-crossed him or filing for bankruptcy, he found a way to pay back the bank.

When he was forced to move from the place he loved so much and did not grow bitter, instead immersing himself in his new community, getting involved at church and in Young Life.

When cancer struck and he did not abandon God, but trusted Him, despite the hurt of having to leave behind those he loved.

His legacy was not the passing of a wooden baton to his children; that was simply the symbol of what had already been given. Wrote his sister, Cathy, after his death: "Chuck left us an example of how to live and how to die....I think our way of paying tribute to Chuck would be to love a little deeper, listen more, complain less, overlook faults, grow in faith, reach out to others, be less selfish, and care more."

"Chuck Austin," wrote one newspaper editorial writer, "clearly believed service to others was as important as service to one's own desires. He believed, further, that such service should be given with a smile and a handshake, not with frowns and lectures. His attitude set him in what has become an unhappily lonely class, that of a true gentleman."

It was written by my crusty old boss.

Now, in the aftermath of the annual Eagles-Austin race, I watch little kids eat watermelon and dive headfirst on slip-and-slides, and runners partake of the free barbecue the church has provided. I meet some of the nearly two dozen relatives of Chuck's who are at the race, representing four generations. And I meet Chuck's father, the man who planted the seeds of faith in his son and, at 91, was planning a spring trip to Ireland to check out his family's roots.

Chuck's oldest son, Steve, now 34, sits on the bumper of his Toyota, holding his one-year-old son, Mathias. Like two of his siblings, Steve is an elementary-school teacher who loves his work and has been a longtime Young Life leader. His younger brother, David, lives in Washington, DC, where he's involved in an array of other-oriented jobs—from working to help orphans in Katmandu be allowed public education to helping organize the National Prayer Breakfast. Connie, Linda, and Lynette, like Steve, are teachers, or going to school to become teachers. They're involved in youth ministry, camps—in short, involved in the lives of young people.

Steve shows me letters he wrote to his father and letters his father wrote to him. Then, from a grocery sack, he suddenly pulls it out: the baton. I hold it, read the words, admire the craftsmanship—layers of hardwoods laminated into oneness.

It is, I sense, a hallowed piece of wood. But someone else is even more infatuated with it than I am. Young Mathias reaches out with tiny fingers and, eyes wide, takes the baton from Steve's hand. He holds it tightly. He examines it. And as his father watches, he joyfully waves it in the air, as if it is his and he will never let it go.

Orphan Tree

For reasons no one is certain of, seeds from the Olympian trees can't gain a foothold in the soil. But there is one place they can grow. The fallen crumbling giants of an earlier forest can nurse logs from fragile seedlings. When the little trees grow strong enough, they send down roots around the log into the soil. From one decaying monarch, many trees can find nourishment.

—*Parables of the Forest*

Every Christmas Eve, we gather at the home of my wife's sister or parents. We mingle. We eat. We make fun of my brother-in-law the culturally challenged doctor, whom we all secretly admire because he doesn't have an answering machine, has never used an ATM, and thinks the Spice Girls have something to do with parsley, sage, rosemary, and thyme.

Then, prior to opening presents, we gather round for what you might call the "program" portion of the evening. Songbooks are passed out. Throats are cleared. Finally, when one of my nieces places her fingers on the piano keys and launches into "Joy to the World," I feel all the pressure of the season and of the whole year instantly leave me, especially when I hear the phrase "...and heav'n and nature sing...."

(You don't hear much about heav'n and nature singing these days, except at Christmas; plus, this is the one time of year you can say "heaven" as if it were one syllable and get away with it.)

There is no sweeter music than the sound of "Joy to the World" played on a piano by one of my nieces on Christmas Eve while three or four generations try desperately to sing in key. It does not matter that each person in that room is different, that some of us have white-collar jobs and some of us have blue, that some of us are old and some of us are young, that some of us root for the University of Oregon and some of us for Oregon State. It does not matter that we're not some sort of stay-pressed family that never wrinkles. It does not matter that, were they in public, some of the singers in this family could be arrested for disturbing the peace (especially my brother-in-law-who-has-never-used-an-ATM).

It is not quality that counts here; it is context. It is praise for God from whom all blessings flow. It is celebration for the greatest gift of all. It is thanksgiving for a family that circles the Christ child like the presents around the tree.

For in these moments we are the essence of oneness, tied together by tradition. And traditions help keep family legacies alive. They help us stay focused on what matters in life—and by the end of the year, our focus can sometimes be pretty fuzzy.

After a few more songs, the younger children will act out the Christmas story (have bathrobe, will travel) or my brother-in-law will read it. Then the lights dim for the drama. The Paul Scandrett Memorial Theater Company, named in honor of my nephew and former shepherd who died at 16, takes the living-room stage.

For seven of the last eight years, we've offered some sort of homemade drama on Christmas Eve. Some of the older children try to pretend that this production is uncool, but secretly they love it, for Christmas is appreciated most, I think, by those who see the world through childlike eyes.

It is a concept rooted in Scripture itself, in Matthew where the disciples ask Jesus who's the greatest in the kingdom of heaven. He does not tell them what some people might tell them today: that the greatest are those who have the most divinity degrees or give the most money to the church or preach the most emotional sermon or memorize the most Bible verses or have the flashiest pro-God bumper stickers.

Instead, Jesus called to a little child and had the child stand among them. And He said, "Unless you change and become like children, you will never enter the kingdom of heaven. Therefore, whoever humbles himself like this child is the greatest in the kingdom of heaven. And whoever welcomes a little child like this in my name welcomes me" (Matthew 18:3-5).

So often, adults think materially and children think spiritually. Langston Hughes, whose African-American poetry plumbed the depths of a race's despair and determination, once wrote a children's book called *Carol of the Brown Child: Nativity Poems*, in which a child wonders what he should bring to the manger. Gifts? Gold? Money? Finally the child says, "I will bring my heart and give my heart to Him. I will bring my heart to the manger."

What Jesus (a guy not big on hypocrites) loved about children wasn't their perfection, but their faith—their willingness to believe even if much remained mysterious to them. Their hearts. Their humility. Their realness.

Which is what makes our living-room drama work: its realness. Each production is perfectly imperfect. But each belongs to us, not Broadway; to Him, not some audience we're trying to please.

I feel the same way about Christmas trees. What I like in a Christmas tree is realness, character, personality. I encountered a perfect Christmas tree once; in fact, I put it together for a drama production at our church. Nothing against those who have artificial trees, but they're not for me. I am a traditionalist and don't believe a tree should come with set-up instructions, say "Made in Thailand," and include seven color-coded, letter-designated levels of branches. It's just not right.

Once when we lived in central Oregon, Sally and I cross-country skied into the woods to find a Christmas tree. We came back dragging the evergreen equivalent of a canine mutt. It was a gnarly, oddly shaped tree that someone had cut and left, perhaps to get at a better one. We've always called it "the orphan tree," because it seemed to be lonely and looking for a home. And I'm glad we gave it one.

Like our Christmas Eve drama production, it took a little imagination (OK, tons of imagination) to see its beauty. But it was there; we just had to look hard enough. To throw off our prejudices about perfect trees. To look at it with childlike eyes.

Imagination fuels our family's Christmas Eves. Tradition imbues them with meaning. But what sustains them year after year—even when there are empty chairs at the dinner table—is a truth that we trust in as a family: that the Christ of the Christmas carols is more than a child in a manger. He is the God of the universe, not some bellhop who scurries to carry our bags when we check in at Christmas and Easter. Whatever legacies we pass on to one another are rooted in the legacy that He passed on to us.

Says Paul in 1 Corinthians 3:6: "I planted the seed, Apollos watered it, but God made it grow." Later, in his letter to the Ephesians, Paul reminds us that we are chosen of God, guaranteed an inheritance, saved by grace; in essence, welcomed in from the cold.

In a sense, we're not unlike that orphan tree: saved despite our shortcomings, brought into a warm home, and given a place of honor. We were chosen not because of our merits, but because of His mercy—the mercy of a God with a heart to welcome the lost and lonely. Chosen not because of who we are, but because of who He is: a God full of grace.

In essence, then, we're His legacies. For after that child in the manger grew up, He healed the blind, stilled the waters, fed the poor, and then was hung on a cross, only to keep the ultimate promise that we commemorate each Easter with what I think are the three most important words in the human language: *He is risen*.

Now He is gone, but He lives on in us, *through* us, in the form of the Holy Spirit. It is a thought that does more than cause me pause; it makes me shudder. It makes me feel like I suppose the shepherds felt on that first Christmas night—a bunch of ragtag guys who, one minute, were abiding in their fields and, the next, were standing in the presence of a monarch, not knowing quite how to act.

They were "sore afraid" until an angel said unto them, "Fear not, for, behold, I bring you good tidings of great joy, which shall be to all people. For unto you is born this day in the city of David a Saviour, which is Christ the Lord" (Luke 2:10,11 KJV).

God looked down on that scene and loved those shepherds as if they were royalty themselves. In His eyes, they were perfect in their imperfection, for they belonged to Him and each had come to that manger with the faith of a child. Sort of like our family gathered around the piano on Christmas Eve, celebrating the blessed event with imperfect notes that must sound perfect only to the audience of One:

> Joy to the world
> The Lord is come
> Let heav'n and nature sing!

The Farm

When conditions are suitable and the seed's outer coat absorbs enough moisture to allow the inside kernel to swell, the seed comes to life and bursts out of its coat. Once the seed sprouts and breaks the surface of the soil, I can't see the seed anymore. It is no more. The seed has given itself to become something larger and more wonderful—a plant that will produce many more seeds.

—*In God's Garden*

As I turn onto the gravel lane, the headlights of my '93 Explorer remind me how deep go the roots of this place. "Century Farm," says the sign. "Youngberg Home Place 1889."

I stop for a moment. Then I head down the road, carefully avoiding the muddy potholes. My middle-age caution triggers remembrances of more rambunctious days. Twenty-five years ago, aboard Pop's tractor, Sally and I would purposely hit every one of those potholes, whooping aloud as we bounced home with her grandparents' mail.

Now, in the farmland of Oregon's Yamhill County, all is quiet on this February night in 1998. Sally is four time zones away, scrubbing the scabies of Third World babies while on a medical mission in the Dominican Republic. Our oldest son, a student at nearby Linfield College, is 18—the same age

I was when I first rode that tractor with his farm-bred mother.

As I approach the house, I see it: the big leaf maple that guards this place like a loyal, if aging, sentry. It had been planted around the turn of the century, old photographs suggest, probably by my wife's great-grandfather, Nels Youngberg, who sailed for America from Sweden in 1882 at age 21 and sent for his bride-to-be, Hannah, soon thereafter.

In its century-long life, the maple has been the tie tree for horses, the backdrop for dozens of family photos, the home base for countless games of hide-and-seek—the silent witness to one family's history.

It was there, in 1923, when Pop came down the lane in what was probably a Model-T to introduce Nels and Hannah to his fiancée, Louise.

In 1949, when Gram and Pop's son Harold came down the lane in his two-tone '47 Chevy, with his fiancée, Bonnie.

In 1972, when Bonnie and Harold's daughter Linda came down the lane in a '68 VW bug with her fiancé, Greg.

And in 1994, when Linda and Greg's daughter Traci, came down the lane in an '81 Jeep with her fiancé, Brandon.

I get out of the car and look at the tree. Its trunk, rutted and splotched with moss, is now nearly as wide as my car.

I half-expect Princie the border collie to wag me a welcome, as if I had just run an errand in town instead of having been gone for nearly a decade since last staying here.

But Princie is gone. Gram is gone. Pop is gone. And looking at the maple is like looking at my mother the first time I realized she was getting old. But as Sally's aunt and uncle welcome me in, I unpack with great expectations, as if my overnight visit will somehow reconnect me with all that was good about this place. As if I will somehow breathe deep the musty fragrance of this farmhouse and forget all that has changed.

I have not been inside more than a few minutes when I begin realizing that home places are hard to find once you've left them behind.

"What are your plans for tomorrow morning?" asks Sally's Aunt Jeanne, who moved into the Home Place with husband, Wayne, after Gram moved to a retirement home.

I tell her I want to explore the farm and maybe cross the creek into the lower pasture to see the firs that Pop had planted back in the sixties. In 1975, he had let Sally and me cut one—our first Christmas tree as husband and wife. I want to see what the remaining trees look like now.

"Good luck," she says. "The flood washed out the bridge two years ago."

It is a reminder that time carves its own course. Time peels the rose-patterned wallpaper off the wall of the guest room I will sleep in this night. It tints the family photos on the dresser with a sickly shade of green. It jolts me in the form of a Lifestyler 8.0 treadmill, complete with an "accusmart motivational fitness monitor" that seems a high-tech intruder in this century-old bedroom.

I'm not here to see the here-today-garage-sale-tomorrow stuff of the world I left. I'm here to find something else, something of permanence. Something that has endured. History.

Around here, it hangs in the air like the dust of a pickup truck rumbling down a dirt road. I'm in the same house where Pop was born and died, a house that his father built 105 years ago; not the deep-rooted architectural history of the South and East, I realize, but well-seasoned for the relatively young West.

How many mornings did Gram and Pop sit across from one another at breakfast in this house and, afterward, listen to one another as she read from the Bible and he from *Our Daily Bread*? How many sunrises dried the dew on Gram's roses? How many sunsets faded in the sky while Pop, on the tractor, worked to beat the dark?

Thousands. Tens of thousands. Day after day: the poetry of life with structured rhythm, so much different from the often-chaotic cadence of my own life.

I go to sleep listening to a clock ticking. In the morning, I throw on jeans, a sweatshirt, and a coat. As Sally's aunt and uncle watch a TV reporter talk about the possibilities of biological warfare, I head out the door to explore. A cold wind from the southeast whips across the farm. It has been a particularly wet, mild winter in the Willamette Valley, a result of El Ninõ, but this day dawns cold and raw.

The garage roof is thick with moss. The chicken shed is dark and quiet, its tenants replaced by pigeons. The road to the lower pasture is waist-high grass and no longer a road to anywhere.

Blackberries cling to the sides of weathered barns like octopus tentacles about to choke their prey. Pop's old workshop is still full of tools that haven't been touched in more than a decade, keys that no longer open doors, bolts and nuts that no longer fasten machinery.

Once these barns were full of cows and chickens. Now cobwebs connect the prongs on a pitchfork, and a tattered feeding schedule hangs from a wall. The schedule is for 4-H animals belonging to Jeanne, the 66-year-old woman who is now inside cleaning up the breakfast dishes. When this schedule was being used, however, she was 14; Pop's pencil-scrawled entries date back to 1945, the year World War II ended.

I look out in the field and remember seeing deer across the way, nibbling in the shadows of the oaks. For a moment, it is all the way it was. I hear Princie barking and evening crickets singing and, back at the house, Gram and Sally husking corn on the front porch, talking and laughing. But the February wind whips me back to the present; a torn strip of aluminum roofing moans in the distance.

The bridge is gone. Across the swollen creek, I see the hillside where we had chosen that Christmas tree. The firs are now perhaps 100 feet tall, with trunks a foot thick—a little large for even the most spacious living room.

I wander a bit more, take two rolls of photographs, then head back to the farmhouse. As I open the gate, I instinctively close it quickly behind me so none of the cows will get out, then realize there *are* no cows to get out; haven't been for more than a decade. Like so much else around here, the gate's purpose belongs to another time. Like the tools in the workshop, it is no longer necessary.

That's what taints my foray back to the farm, what spoils the quiet like that strip of aluminum roofing that grates on my mind: the idea that all this was somehow for naught, that not only are these tools and tractors and greenhouses no longer needed, but the lives of those who drove those tractors and watered those plants—Gram and Pop—were just as unnecessary.

Maybe it was a mistake to come, I wonder. To think that I would find whatever it was I was looking for. Regardless, it is time to leave.

In the living room, Sally's aunt taps away on a computer; writing to missionaries around the world, she says. I zip my duffel bag and take one last look at a room that time has forgotten, save for the Lifestyler 8.0 treadmill, which looks as out-of-place this morning as it did last night.

I'm heading out the bedroom door when I see it: a notebook that sits on the treadmill's book stand. It is, I assume, the handwriting of Sally's aunt. I stop to read it:

> Bless those who persecute you, bless and do not curse. Rejoice with those who rejoice; mourn with those who mourn. Live in harmony with one another. Do not be proud, but be willing to

> associate with people of low position. Do not be conceited. Do not repay anyone evil for evil. Be careful to do what is right in the eyes of everybody. If it is possible, as far as it depends on you, live at peace with everyone (Romans 12:14-18).

The idea emerges slowly, like the heat from a wood stove, then ignites: I had been thinking all wrong. In my quest to find continuance, I had been searching in all the wrong places. The legacy of The Farm isn't found in barns and tractors and fields. Not in things, but in people still living, words still inspiring, values still being practiced. Not in tools lying in that shed, but in tools that were passed on to us long ago by Gram and Pop: tools to build lives.

The legacy of this place, I realize, lives on when my wife's Aunt Jeanne steps on that newfangled treadmill and, to help her memorize Scripture, rewrites the words that were Gram and Pop's daily bread, and e-mails encouragement to lonely missionaries around the world. Because it was Gram and Pop who helped teach her we should encourage one another.

It lives on in another generation: when Sally and her sister, Ann, embraced Milandé, a Dominican child burned in an accident and, in so doing, mourned with those who mourn. Because it was Gram and Pop who helped teach their son Harold—and his daughters Sally and Ann—courage and compassion.

And it lives on in yet another generation: when Ann's daughter Carrie, at 16, had the courage to go to Haiti with her father to help the sick and the poor. And when my son Ryan had the compassion to be at the side of his great-grandmother in the days before she died. When Gram took a turn for the worse and had to be hospitalized, other family members were unavailable. Told of the situation, Ryan, Linfield Class of 2001, went to be with his Gram, Linfield Class of 1924, so she would not be alone.

All of which makes me think back to what my brother-in-law Greg had said at the memorial service, about how we are Gram's legacy; we are what's left to show the world who she was. And who Pop was, as well.

Legacies live on from generation to generation with a subtlety that makes them easy to miss: the ever-recurring cycle repeating itself silently and ceaselessly, through birth, growth, maturity, death, and decay.

They live on like the wind that tickles the leaves of the massive maple: a gentle force sent by those we can no longer see, rustling our souls in ways we might not fully know, and promising to rustle the souls of those who follow.

Those winds are at work in Michele, a five-year-old great-granddaughter of Gram and Pop's, who, at Gram's memorial service, presented a short letter and picture she had drawn. "I love you gramma," said the letter to the woman who had written so many herself, "and I always will. Have a good time in heaven."

And those winds are at work in Sally's cousin Ron, when he finds himself waving to departing guests until they're completely out of sight, because Gram and Pop always did that for him and his family when they would come visit. He says he has no idea what it means to his guests; he only knows that it seems the right way to say good-bye, and so he carries on what he calls "a ritual of friendship and respect."

And those winds are at work in hundreds of other ways that we'll only notice if we slow down and concentrate on what really matters in this life.

For now, it's time to say good-bye to The Farm. I bid farewell to Sally's aunt and uncle, get in the car, and circle around the maple. I'm just about to round the bend and head down the gravel lane when I see it: the new addition. I had missed it on my way in the previous night in the dark.

I stop the car and look. We had dedicated it at the Fourth of July reunion back in 1994: a tiny maple tree. Dozens of the

75 people at the reunion had gathered round while Sally's father rolled Gram and her wheelchair into position. He took her wrinkled hands and helped her grasp the shovel. Then, together, mother and son scooped the first blade of rich Oregon soil into a pre-dug hole, and the cheering and clapping began.

Family member after family member—adults, kids, four generations in all—took turns shoveling soil into a spot where someday, we hoped, roots would grow deep.

Now, four years later, it is still a twig compared with even some of the branches of the nearby big leaf. On this winter day, the new tree's branches look as stark as the fields that flank it, sparse calligraphy against a pewter-gray sky.

But if the sentry on the other side of the house symbolizes this family's rootedness to the past, the spindly infant symbolizes something, too. It takes only a little imagination to consider that a century ago, the big leaf probably looked much like this one, and that few probably paused to consider how great it one day would be.

Considering that, the infant no longer looks as frail as I previously thought. In fact, as I look back one last time from inside the Explorer, I see its branches reach toward heaven with a hint of hopefulness, a touch of possibility—a promise of many springs to come.

Epilogue

The forest is forever in the process of becoming.

—*A Forest of Voices*

The family that used to live next door once signed all their names in a slab of wet driveway cement. When the cement dried, their names and the year they had signed them were permanently fixed—and still are. But since then, the family has fractured; the mother and father got divorced, each remarried, and the two teenage kids went their separate ways.

Words—even those all but cast in stone—don't freeze life in a permanent pose. They simply reflect the way it was at the time you wrote them. And so it is with this book. Much has changed since I began writing eight months ago; some for the good, some not.

Soon after the death of Grandpa Schu, his beloved apple trees along 30th Street were cut down at the SAE fraternity where the two of us had worked together during my boyhood summers. Like Schu, they had grown old and diseased. But I still see them as I drive by, and I still see a gray-haired man in well-pressed beige pants with cuffs, a long-sleeve shirt, and steel-shanked boots.

Gifty, the little girl adopted from Liberia, is a second-grader at the country school she attends, and reads at or above her grade level. She has a bent for drama and, along with her pal and sister Suzanne, knows virtually every line of *Parent Trap*.

Oscar Hernandez has bought a defunct restaurant and is remodeling it. He plans to open his second restaurant soon.

In Colorado, Lynn and Arie Van Wingerden have adopted their twenty-third child: a three-year-old Korean boy with cerebral palsy. Two of their older children have gotten married. And their first grandchild, a girl named Ashley, was recently born.

I sent the letter to the father whom I wrote of in "The Empty Chair." He wrote back and said I didn't understand him or his son. He had tried everything and nothing worked. It was his son's fault, he wrote, not his.

Meanwhile, my wife's herd of cows is threatening to burst the barn. Among her latest creations is the cow angel (we're among the few houses that has a guardian udder).

Ryan, now a college sophomore, often drives to my old hometown, Corvallis, to see his girlfriend, who attends college there—exactly what I did 25 years ago to see his mother. Stranger yet, the kid sleeps in my old bedroom while staying with his grandmother. One difference between us: His car has reverse.

Jason, a high school sophomore, has guided his computer football team to a 53-2 record and won four Super Bowl titles since I began the book. We've grown closer, in part because we've spent the last six months side by side in an office only slightly larger than a java hut. Last week he actually read one of the book's chapters, and I learned the "122 Z D Post, X D Dig"—a pass play that he says is unstoppable, but I think my headless linebackers could thwart with ease.

In June, two months after my mother and I launched the sailboat together for the first time since my father's death, she was among 15 passengers aboard a 60-foot ship exploring the Galapagos Islands off Ecuador. It was near sunset and, though the sea wasn't particularly choppy, the ship seemed unstable to some aboard.

Suddenly, a wave slammed against the ship. The vessel capsized and quickly sank. In the gathering darkness, one man, hanging to a life ring, said good-bye and slipped underwater. Three others drowned, too. My mother swam from the overcrowded life ring to a wooden life raft and hung to its side. Two hours later, she and the others were rescued by a passing ship. The story made national TV.

Me? I bought a new clock radio. It works wonderfully, though it doesn't do nearly the job nature does in reminding me of life's changes.

When I began this book, the dogwood in front of my house was in full pink blossom. Since then, it has slipped on a summer vest of green, donned a claret-colored back-to-school outfit, and is now adorned in multicolored Christmas lights, nine leaves grudgingly hanging on like a ragtag baseball team being replaced by a bunch of glitzy all-stars.

Amid such change, we endure. We grow. And we come to know what to carry on the journey and what to leave behind. After nearly drowning in that shipwreck, my mother, now 71, said she has no plans to step foot on an oceangoing ship anytime soon.

However, she is already planning a trip this summer to explore the San Juan Islands in Washington state. She starts her sea-kayak lessons soon.

Author's Notes

In making the link between the human experience and nature, a number of books on trees, gardening, and farming enlightened me greatly. Among them:

Chris Anderson and Lex Runciman, editors, *A Forest of Voices* (Mountain View, CA: Mayfield Publishing, 1995). Excerpt from "A Life in Our Hands" by Keith Ervin.

Jennifer Bennett, *Our Gardens Ourselves: Reflections on an Ancient Art* (Buffalo, NY: Camden House, 1994).

Wendell Berry, *The Wheel* (San Francisco: North Point Press, 1982).

Bernd Henrich, *The Trees in My Forest* (New York: Cliff Street Books, 1997).

Gerald Jonas, *North American Trees* (Pleasantville, NY: Reader's Digest, 1993).

Andy and Katie Lipkis, *The Simple Act of Planting a Tree* (Los Angeles: Jeremy P. Tarcher, Inc., 1990).

Jake Page and the editors of Time-Life Books, *Forest* (Alexandria, VA: Time-Life Books, 1983).

E. C. Pielou, *The World of Northern Evergreens* (Ithaca, NY: Comstock Publishers Associates, 1988).

Rutherford Platt, *1001 Questions Answered About Trees* (New York: Dodd, Mead & Co., 1959).

Pamela Reeve, *Parables of the Forest* (Sisters, OR: Multnomah Press, 1989).

Joyce Sackett, *In God's Garden* (Wheaton, IL: Tyndale House, 1998).

Henry Thoreau, *Faith in a Seed: The Dispersion of Seeds and Other Late Natural History Writings*, edited by Bradley P. Dean (Washington, DC: Island Press, 1996).

Carol Williams, *Bringing a Garden to Life* (New York: Bantam Books, 1998).

Also from Bob Welch...

A Father for All Seasons

A great book for every man who wants to father well.

—STU WEBER, AUTHOR OF *TENDER WARRIOR*

Welch's prose will bring a lump
to the throat of any mom reading it. A+.

—CHRISTIAN PARENTING

Full of emotion, meaning, laughter and tears,
and will connect with readers on a deep level.

—GARY SMALLEY, *TODAY'S FAMILY*

Bob Welch has done in A Father for All Seasons
what we all would be wise to do—stop, reflect, learn,
and appreciate all that we have as sons and fathers.

—STEVE LARGENT, MEMBER OF CONGRESS

Get ready for a pleasant journey into self-reflection
and useful insights.

—JOHN FISCHER, AUTHOR/SONGWRITER

Bob Welch has written a small jewel of a book.

—WILLIAM TAAFFE, FORMER *SPORTS ILLUSTRATED* EDITOR